MONTANA'S
FUR TRADE ERA

F. Lee Graves

Montana Magazine and
American & World Geographic Publishing

LEE KAISER

Above: *After wading for hours in a cold mountain stream, the fur trapper looked forward to warming by the fire reflecting on his day's activities. His Dutch-oven style cooking pot often yielded buffalo roast or stewed beaver tail, both considered delicacies.*

Title page: *"Full Packs," by Montana artist Robert F. Morgan.*
COURTESY OF ROBERT F. MORGAN

Front cover: *Thomas Erskine Dawson (born October 6, 1859, at Fort Benton; died November 1953) was a scout, trader, and homesteader in northern Montana. He was the son of Andrew Dawson, one of the owners of the American Fur Company. His mother was a Gros Ventre, Pipe Woman. The artist, Winold Reiss, was commissioned by Great Northern Railway to do portraits of Indians for the "Great Northern Art Calendar," first in 1927.*
MONTANA HISTORICAL SOCIETY,
BEQUEST OF HELENE EDKINS, WINOLD REISS

Back cover, top: *Red Lodge Rendezvous.* ROBERT KELLEHER PHOTO
Back cover, bottom: *Missouri River near Three Forks.*
WAYNE MUMFORD PHOTO

Foreword

Fur trappers and traders played an important part in the story of the West. Two hundred years ago, the journals and oral tradition of the first explorers, fur trappers, and traders interested many other people in the exploration of the West and its entrepreneurial possibilities. A new breed of men resulted who, in most cases, left comfortable surroundings for the danger of lands unknown, seeking their fortunes and adventure. I hope to relate the fur-trade story geographically to an area with which the reader is familiar, as well as show the importance of the fur era and delineate its impact today. I hope to tell interesting stories that show human nature and relate to us because we generally all value comfortable shelter, good food, a safe environment, a good story and a challenge. References to locations usually will reflect modern names rather than those of the time. For example, Idaho and Montana are used as geographical areas, but did not become reality until 1863 and 1864 respectively.

Acknowledgments

I would like to thank several persons for help and support for this book. My wife, Carol, a true artist in her own right, has been my co-photographer, proofreader, gentle and persistent critic, and more important, constant companion. Jack and Susan Lepley of Fort Benton opened their home and donated a Sunday to us that deepened our insight into the Fort Benton story. Jack's tour of several old fort sites along the Missouri was full of great history and good tales and helped to make the story more real. Gary Roedl, Spokane, and Rod Wamsley, Charlo, of the Fort Connah Association helped a lot with researching the fur trade in general and Fort Connah in particular. Richard Boyd and Charles Rankin of the Montana Historical Society were very helpful with books and references. Dr. Dale Tash of Dillon gave much sought-after advice about the fur trade that was put to practical use. Dr. Tash's editing of the text was also appreciated. *Montana Magazine*'s Barbara Fifer and Teresa Record were great to work with and offered much time and support for the project. A very special thanks goes to Paul Hedren, Superintendent of Fort Union National Historic Site, who donated the best part of a very beautiful September day to give Carol and me a personal tour that resulted in a greater understanding of the place of Fort Union in Montana's early history as well as yielding many good photographs. As with any project, the team effort is what makes it successful; many thanks to you all!

Library of Congress Cataloging-in-Publication Data
Graves, F. Lee.
  Montana's fur trade era / F. Lee Graves.
    p.   cm.
  Includes bibliographical references (p.) and index
  ISBN 1-56037-054-8
  1. Fur trade–Montana–History. 2. Fur traders–Montana–History. 3. Montana–History. 4. Montana–Geography.
F731.G73 1994   94-11761
978.6'01–dc20

Write for our catalog:
American & World Geographic Publishing,
P.O. Box 5630, Helena, MT 59604

Printed in U.S.A. by Fenske Companies, Billings, Montana

CONTENTS

ERWIN AND PEGGY BAUER PHOTOS

Beaver (Castor canadensis*) was called the currency of the mountains and was one of the main reasons for the early exploration and settling of western North America.*

A beaver house, home to many beavers at once, signalled the trappers to beaver presence. The house is so well built that for it to be dismantled by humans, it must be taken apart stick by stick or blown apart with dynamite. This excellent example is in Wyoming's Tetons.

Montana Fur Posts

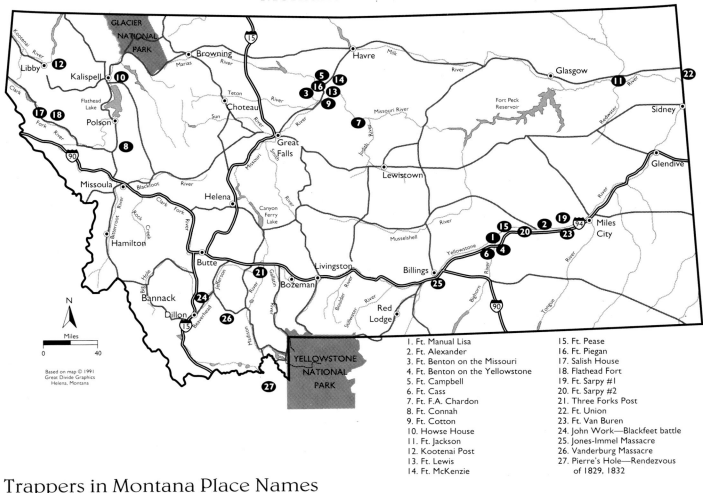

1. Ft. Manual Lisa
2. Ft. Alexander
3. Ft. Benton on the Missouri
4. Ft. Benton on the Yellowstone
5. Ft. Campbell
6. Ft. Cass
7. Ft. F.A. Chardon
8. Ft. Connah
9. Ft. Cotton
10. Howse House
11. Ft. Jackson
12. Kootenai Post
13. Ft. Lewis
14. Ft. McKenzie
15. Ft. Pease
16. Ft. Piegan
17. Salish House
18. Flathead Fort
19. Ft. Sarpy #1
20. Ft. Sarpy #2
21. Three Forks Post
22. Ft. Union
23. Ft. Van Buren
24. John Work—Blackfeet battle
25. Jones-Immel Massacre
26. Vanderburg Massacre
27. Pierre's Hole—Rendezvous of 1829, 1832

Based on map © 1991
Great Divide Graphics
Helena, Montana

Trappers in Montana Place Names

Ashley Creek	Flathead County. Joe Ashley, a trader who worked for Angus McDonald of North West Co.
Bridger	Town in Carbon County. Free trapper and Rocky Mountain Fur Co. partner, James Bridger.
Choteau	Pierre Chouteau, Jr., president of the American Fur Company. The town chose to drop the letter "u" in the name. County seat of Teton County.
Chouteau County	Auguste and Pierre Chouteau of the American Fur Company.
Culbertson	County seat of Roosevelt County. Alexander Culbertson, American Fur Company leader.
Dawson County	Andrew Dawson of the American Fur Company.
Fort Benton	Missouri Senator Thomas Hart Benton, fur-trade supporter.
Gardiner, Montana Gardner River	Recorded both as "Johnson Gardiner" and as "Johnston Gardner," this free trapper of the region in the 1830s is memorialized either way.
Grant	Possibly named for Hudson's Bay Company trapper Major Richard Grant, who retired in 1855 and settled in the area.
Jocko River/Valley	Named for Jacques "Jocko" Finlay of the North West Company and Hudson's Bay Company.
McDonald	Lake in Glacier Park possibly named for family of Angus and Duncan McDonald.
Pease Bottom	F.D. Pease, trader and Indian agent. A small valley near Hysham.
Ross's Hole	Alexander Ross, North West Company brigade leader.
Sarpy Creek Sarpy Basin	Big Horn County. John B. Sarpy, a member of the prominent St. Louis fur-trade family.
Thompson Falls	David Thompson of the North West Company.
Tullock Creek	Big Horn County. Samuel Tullock of the American Fur Company.

Fur Trade Chronology

1670	Hudson's Bay Company chartered by British crown; first on North American continent.
1743	Verendrye party probably first white men to see Montana.
1783	North West Company organized.
1801-02	Charles LeRaye as Indian captive explores Big Horn and Yellowstone and winters on Stillwater near Big Timber.
1804-06	Lewis and Clark Expedition.
1805	Larocque explores Big Horn Canyon and Yellowstone River.
1806-07	Joseph Dickson, explorer and trapper, winters in Montana and traps Yellowstone.
1807	Fort Manuel Lisa first permanent settlement in Montana (November).
1808	St. Louis, Missouri Fur Company organized.
	Kootenai Post built by North West Company near Libby.
	American Fur Company organized by J.J. Astor in New York.
	"Colter's Run" at Three Forks motivated by Blackfeet.
1809	Salish House established by North West Company's David Thompson near Libby.
1810	Henry's Post built near Three Forks by Missouri Fur Company.
	April 30: George Drouillard and two others killed at Three Forks by Blackfeet.
	Howse House built near Kalispell by Hudson's Bay Company.
1812	Thompson surveys Missoula area from Mount Jumbo.
1816	Congress passes the act that excludes foreigners from participating in the fur trade in the United States and its territories.
1818	The 49th parallel becomes the U.S.-Canadian boundary east of the Rocky Mountains.
1821	English Parliament passes an act that excludes all American traders from Canadian territory.
	Pilcher of Missouri Fur Company establishes Fort Benton on the Yellowstone.
	Hudson's Bay Company and North West Company consolidated.
1822	Rocky Mountain Fur Company founded at St. Louis.
1823	Jones-Immel Massacre by Blackfeet near Billings.
	American Fur Company's Western Department created, based in St. Louis.
1825	First of annual rendezvous in the mountains.
1829	Fort Union established by American Fur Company near the confluence of the Missouri and Yellowstone rivers.
1831	Kipp builds Fort Piegan near mouth of Marias River for Blackfeet trade. Abandoned in the fall.
1832	Fort Cass erected by Tullock for American Fur Company for Crow trade.
	Fort McKenzie built near Fort Piegan for Blackfeet trade.
	Congress passes a law prohibiting alcohol in Indian territories.
	The steamboat *Yellow Stone* reaches Fort Union.
1834	Rocky Mountain Fur Company holds its last rendezvous and is dissolved.
	Astor retires from fur trade. Pratt, Chouteau and Company buy out Western Department of the American Fur Company.
1837	Small pox devastates Blackfeet near Three Forks.
1840	Last rendezvous by American Fur Company.
1843	Fort McKenzie burned.
	John James Audubon visits Fort Union and Montana and leaves a legacy of his paintings and journals.
1844	Fort Chardon established at the Judith River.
1845	Fort Lewis replaces Fort Chardon upriver.
	Fort Campbell built of adobe.
1846	Fort Benton on Missouri established by Alexander Culbertson.
	49th parallel established as border with Canada to the Pacific Ocean.
1850	First adobe building at Fort Benton.
1859	Adobe Fort Benton completed.
1860	First steamboat, *Chippewa*, arrives at levee at Fort Benton.
1868	Last year Fort Benton used as a fur fort.
1966	Fort Union National Trading Post established as a unit in the National Park Service System.

The Influence of the Early Explorers

Montana prior to the Lewis and Clark Expedition was largely uncharted and unreported except for the sketchy reports of a few brave explorers who ventured into the area. The first reports of white men to see Montana were those of the Verendrye brothers, Louis-Joseph and François, who saw "a land of shining mountains" on New Year's Day of 1743. Whether they saw the Big Horns of Montana and Wyoming or the Black Hills of South Dakota is still disputed. Most historians believe, however, that it was distant Montana (a Latin derivative meaning mountainous) sighted on that crisp winter day.

Many explorers followed in the next sixty years prior to the United States' Louisiana Purchase from France for $15 million, which extended U.S. territory closer to the Pacific Ocean. The theory of a waterway, a Northwest Passage, from the east coast's Atlantic Ocean or from the Mississippi River to the Pacific Ocean kept the uncharted expanse of the now northwest United States alive in the hearts and minds of the adventurous. Rivers are roads that move, and commercially the Northwest Passage would be invaluable. Many expeditions were formed to search for the mythical waterway as well as to trade with the Indians. Fortunately, many explorers kept detailed journals or diaries of their exploits, which ultimately stirred the imaginations of followers to dreams of riches or becoming famous as discoverers of uncharted realms and peoples. Men like French trader Jacques D'Eglise (in Spain's service) explored the Upper Missouri in 1792 with the purpose of furthering trade with the Indians.

Charles LeRaye left Canada in 1801 with goods to trade for furs on the Upper Missouri and began his ascent of the river the third week in September. On October 23, 1801, he was captured by Brule Sioux and taken to their main camp on the Kansas River. He was befriended by a French trader named Pardo who talked the Brule into letting LeRaye go with him to see the family of Pardo's Indian wife at the Hidatsa villages at the mouth of the Knife River in North Dakota. Some of his captors accompanied them. At the Hidatsa village, the party decided "to go to the Yellowstone, and to the Rocky Mountains," and left July 3, 1802 in a westbound party of about 50 people including women and children, and 39 horses. In spite of the size and makeup of the group, they made good time, reaching the Powder River July 10. They followed the Powder River to its mouth on the Yellowstone, near the present site of Terry, where they camped and fished for three days, especially noting fine catches of pike and catfish. The party explored the area of south-central Montana and northern Wyoming, eventually returning to the Hidatsa in North Dakota. LeRaye spent the next few years still in captivity, finally escaping in the spring of 1805 to St. Louis and not ever returning to the Upper Missouri.

Besides Lewis and Clark, the explorer most given credit for making known to the world the various rich resources of the West was François Antoine Larocque of the North West Company of Great Britain. In the spring of 1805 he and his small party of "two white men and some Indians" left the Mandan villages of North Dakota and traveled up the Yellowstone and Powder rivers searching for beaver-trapping potential and intending to trade for skins from the local Indians met along the way.

From the Powder they crossed overland to near present-day Sheridan, Wyoming, and headed north, entering Montana again about August 17, 1805. Larocque reached Pass Creek, which he followed to the junction of the Little Big Horn near Wyola, Montana. At this point in the trip, he joined his Crow companions in a foray against an unnamed tribe of enemies, and noted a particularly gory

Facing page: Woodbine Falls in Carbon County.
F. LEE GRAVES

7

fight. After the battle, his group journeyed across country to War Man Creek, which they followed to the Big Horn River (now at Yellowtail Dam near Hardin). Larocque thoroughly explored the Big Horn Canyon on the Big Horn River and graphically recorded his profound impressions of its rock formations and the immense view northward toward the Yellowstone River. His vantage point was near Pretty Eagle Point.

The party continued up Pryor Creek near Billings, and on September 15, 1805, Larocque recorded in his journal what would later be called Pompey's Pillar, noting a pictograph depicting a battle. All along the way he asked the Crows he met about fur-trapping possibilities and always received favorable answers. He returned to his base of Fort de la Bosse in Manitoba, Canada, with over 125 beaver skins as well as numerous skins of other animals. His journals literally advertised the prime beaver country of the Yellowstone, Big Horn and Powder river regions of Montana and northern Wyoming.

The Lewis and Clark Expedition, 1804 to 1806, also recorded their exploits in detailed journals that often mention the rich abundance of beaver and other fur-bearing animals. Following the expedition, several members, including George Drouillard, John Potts and John Colter, returned to the Northwest and were active in the trade.

Montana in 1806

Lewis and Clark passed through Montana in 1806 on their way back to St. Louis on the final leg of their expedition. Larocque was making his circuitous tour of the Yellowstone. Vast buffalo herds dominated the plains and were constantly hunted by Indian tribes for varied and integral contributions to their lives and very existence. Deer and elk roamed the vast prairies and plains of what in another 83 years would become the forty-first state of the Union. Rivers and creeks meandered lazily in the summer, abounding with fish, muskrat, beaver and otter. Many bodies of water froze solid in winter demanding that any forms of life existing in the watery habitat leave those frozen climes, become encased in an icy prison, or adapt.

Indian tribes or tribal subgroups lived generally around lakes and streams where water was accessible for daily life. They also hunted the immediate area knowing that eventually animals would come to the water to drink. No sprawling towns or ribbons of interstate highway or threads of powerlines meandered over the countryside as yet. The most accessible white settlement was St. Louis, which was a sprawling town of about 1,500 people. Up to 1806, only a handful of white people had experienced life in Montana. The Upper Missouri was beginning to change and would never be the same again. Lewis and Clark reported that in August, when the expedition was returning to St. Louis, they met eleven different parties en route up the Missouri River in

Buffalo or bison (Bison bison) was food and shelter to the fur trappers and traders of the West as well as to the American Indian. Large animals often weigh as much as 2,000 pounds and stand six feet high. Only 1,000 animals remained in 1900 after they were hunted nearly to extinction. Today, nearly 40,000 roam national parks and a few private reserves.

F. LEE GRAVES

Autumn along the Musselshell River near Ryegate, Montana, is a beautiful time in the mountains. During the fall, the beaver fur became thicker and richer for the impending winter, which increased its quality.

search of furs. The Indians eagerly sought the trade goods of Europe and America and placed greatest value on the gun. Their willingness to trade led to activation of the barter system that was long used in intertribal trading. Furs, of course, were the main items the whites wanted from the Indians, and a new era of commerce began.

A chronological account often results in confusion about the various companies and especially the players, many of whom worked at different times for different companies during their careers. Therefore, each company will be studied separately, listing its principal players, achievements and contributions.

Trade Beads

The Indians had valued beads long before the white man introduced glass beads. They used shells, rocks, antler, bone, teeth and even wood, which they strung on sinew or rawhide thongs. When Europeans arrived in North America, the ornaments they wore impressed the Indians. It was not long before the whites traded beads for desired Indian possessions. The bright colors especially impressed the Indians. The trade beads' deep reds, blues, greens and yellows lasted longer on clothing of the Indians than did dyed porcupine quills or painted designs. Beads also were made of copper and brass, but the multicolored glass ones were of much more value to the Indians. Beads were sold in bulk, by weight, string, or individually.

Trade beads came from different places in the world. Many glass beads traded on the North American continent up until the middle of the 19th century were made in the glass factories of Murano, Venice. The deep red beads with whitish centers are called "Cornaline d'Aleppo," or simply cornalines, from their place of origin in Aleppo, Syria. Some beads were named for the company that marketed them, such as the Hudson's Bay Yellow Hearts. Seed beads were multicolored and as small as seeds. Sinew, which is strong and can be made extremely fine, was ideal for stringing seed beads.

Tube beads are also called "cut beads" because they were made originally in the shape of a straw and cut to lengths up to one-quarter inch. Polychrome beads—also called fancy beads, or *millefiore* (Medieval Italian for "thousand flowers")—are a general class and have a multitude of bright colors and designs. The Crow Indians especially valued these fancy beads. Lewis and Clark reported in their journals that the most valued of all beads were the deep-blue beads often referred to as chief beads, denoting the superiority of the ornament, not that they were worn only by the chiefs of a tribe.

1 METAL CONES: USED AS FRINGE
2 a. BRASS TRADE BEADS
   b. TUBE BEADS
   c. BLUE "CHIEF" BEADS; PADRE BEADS
   d. WHITE BONE BEADS
   e. WHITE GLASS BEADS
   f. CORNALINE D'ALEPPO
   g. BONE BEAD
   H. LARGE TAPERED TUBE TRADE BEAD
3 LARGE "CHIEF" BEADS
4 BLUE-GREEN MILLIFIORE
5 BLUE CHEVRON BEADS (EARLY 1800S)

6 AFRICAN MARRIAGE BEAD
7 a. CHINESE COBALT DRAGON EYE
   b. MEDIUM BLUE CHEVRON
   c. THIN GREEN CHEVRON
   D. HUDSON'S BAY YELLOW HEART (EARLY 1600S); ALSO CALLED TUBULAR CROW MEDICINE BEADS
   e. TUBULAR YELLOW FANCY OR MOSAIC BEAD; MILLIFIORE
   f. YELLOW TUBULAR BEAD
   g. WHITE TUBULAR MOSAIC GLASS BEAD
   h. RUSSIAN TRADE BEADS

i. RED FEATHER BEADS

j. MEDIUM BLUE CHEVRON

8 a. BLUE PONY BEADS

  b. VENETIAN TRAIL BEADS (1700s)

9 a. BLUE DISK TRADE BEADS

  B. RED FEATHER BEAD

10 ASSORTED TRADE BEADS (MID-1800s)

11 a. SMALL CORNALINE D'ALEPPO BEADS

  b. CORNALINE D'ALEPPO

12 a. THOUSAND EYES BEADS, BLACK (1700s)

  b. GREEN EYE BEADS (1700s)

  c. THOUSAND EYES BEADS, RED (1700s)

13 AMBER BEADS

14 YELLOW FANCY BEAD

15 RED FEATHER BEAD

16 BLACK OVAL FANCY BEAD

17 BLUE OVAL FANCY BEAD

18 TWO STRANDS OF SEED BEADS

19 YELLOW TUBULAR BEAD

20 BLACK OVAL FANCY BEAD

21 SPIRAL POLYCHROME BEAD (1600s)

22 VENETIAN CORNALINE D'ALEPPO (EARLY 1800s)

23 FOSSILIZED-MASTODON BEADS

Left: *Bitterroot* (Lewisia rediviva) *is the Montana state flower, its scientific name honoring Meriwether Lewis. The pinks and pure whites of the bitterroot were noted by many chroniclers of the early West.* F. LEE GRAVES
Below: *The end of the day on the "Wide Missouri."* LEE KAISER

British Fur Companies

North West Company

The North West Company was formed in 1783 and eventually controlled the fur trade from the Great Lakes to the Pacific Ocean. These Nor'Westers largely were no more than an association of enterprising men agreeing among themselves to carry on the fur trade and remain unattached to any other business concern. They were more energetic and innovative than the longer established and more conservative Hudson's Bay Company; by the year 1800 the North West Company had over 4,000 trappers and traders in the field. Company headquarters were at Montreal, and their posts and trading houses were scattered throughout the West.

Several trading and supply posts eventually were located strategically in Idaho and Montana. The North West Company sent many expeditions to explore and open trade with various tribes of Indians. Francois Antoine Larocque's expedition in 1805 was organized primarily to win the favor and trade of the Crows and Sioux.

In 1808 David Thompson traded and trapped extensively along the Kootenai River in northwest Montana in the areas of Troy, Libby and Lake Koocanusa. Coming from Kootenai House near present-day Canal Flats, Alberta, he became the first white man to enter western Montana by the route across the 49th parallel, which later would become the border between the United States and Canada. He and his men found game and fish scarce in northwest Montana and nearly starved to death. Finally they killed a mountain lion. But before they voraciously consumed the feline, Thompson measured it and noted its characteristics in his journal, a true scientist to be sure.

Thompson sent his trusted subordinate, Finan McDonald, and several of his men to the Flathead Valley to trade with the Kootenai tribe. At the same time, Mc-Donald established a small post, probably only a couple of buildings, called the Kootenai Post, near present-day Libby.

"Network" is a useful term to describe the position of the North West Company at this time, their trading posts and houses strategically located in the vital areas in relation to the rivers and streams and Indian tribes. The area of northwest Montana and northern Idaho looked so promising that Thompson returned in 1809, crossed the mountains again, and built the Kullyspell House on the east shore of Lake Pend Oreille. From this base of operations, he journeyed southeast up the Clark's Fork of the Columbia and in November 1809 built Salish House* near Thompson Falls, with Finan McDonald in charge as chief factor (trader). Jacques, or Jocko, Finlay was also a major trader for Thompson in the area, and for whom the Jocko River and Valley are named.

Salish House was a sturdy cabin built of timber from locally abundant larch and fir trees. Here, Thompson and his small group wintered in the beautiful wide valley of the Clark's Fork River. Thompson also traveled farther west and built the Spokane House on the Spokane River near present-day Spokane, Washington. From the Kullyspell House and Spokane House, the North West Company also gained a firmer foothold *east* of the Rockies. Thompson spent the next few years furthering the aims of the North West Company in the profitable region.

As trading prospered, he was able to indulge more in his favorite pastime—charting and mapping. He journeyed to Astoria, Oregon, mapping all the way, and spent some time with the rival Americans, perhaps to spy on their activities. He returned to the Salish House in November of 1811 and spent the winter.

In February 1812 Thompson visited a

*Salish (also Saleesh) House is the name of two fur posts in northwest Montana. For simplicity, the name Salish House here is used for the North West Company's post and the name Flathead Post for the Hudson's Bay Company's, which is consistent with other sources.

Liquor and the Trade

Distilled spirits, particularly whiskey and rum, played an important role in the fur trade. Both the American and the British companies used liquor as an inducement for the Indians to trade with them. Fur trade historian Hiram Martin Chittenden describes liquor as "the most powerful weapon which the traders could employ in their struggles with one another." The North West Company quickly decided that liberal use of alcohol greatly increased Indians' productivity. The Hudson's Bay Company and American companies were forbidden to use alcohol in trading, but both sides used it unsparingly when competition was keen. Liquor was normally smuggled in, often in barrels of flour, and even freighted around government liquor checkpoints on the Missouri River, such as Leavenworth, Kansas, and Bellevue, Nebraska.

In the summer of 1832 the United States Congress forbade the importation of alcohol into "Indian country." This act caused the Americans to lose an effective bargaining weapon for the Indian fur trade and cost them many furs that went to the British. Kenneth McKenzie, the bourgeois at Fort Union, was so distraught at this new law that he made a visit to Washington, D.C., in January 1833 to persuade the politicians to reconsider the use of liquor near Hudson's Bay posts. He was unsuccessful. He returned to Fort Union, and made a decision. The government forbade the importation of alcohol *into* Indian country, but not its manufacture there. (The same steamboat that brought his brand new distillery that summer also brought Prince Maximilian and Karl Bodmer.)

McKenzie would follow the law—to the letter! He set up a still at Fort Union and soon produced some of the best "corn squeezin's" ever made. News of McKenzie's efforts did not take long to reach official ears. The government gave serious thought to suspending the Upper Missouri Outfit's trading license. However, through the efforts of "friends in high places," such as Secretary of War Lewis Cass, the threat diminished. McKenzie lost his still, but continued to import the liquor so necessary to maintain the balance of trade competition in the field. Liquor was continually used in the trade by both the Americans and the British, but it appears mostly to have been when competition dictated it.

As for the "liquor," it was watered down consistently, and "recipes" varied with those involved in the trade. A popular recipe: To one gallon of liquor, add one gallon of water. Season with cayenne pepper to make it hot. Since whiskey should make the drinker sick, add gall from a buffalo. When a pinch of strychnine is available, add it to give the heart a "jump." Use tobacco to add color and flavor to the mix.

Trapper clad in a capote made from a Hudson's Bay blanket stops exploring to give his horse a rest and to check beaver-trapping possibilities.
LEE KAISER

Flathead camp at the mouth of the Jocko River. He traveled up the Clark's Fork and recorded in his journal on February 25, 1812, that he was in the vast valley of Missoula. Thompson and his party climbed Mt. Jumbo and mapped the Missoula Valley with great precision. A few days later, he and his party headed north and became the first white men to record the view of Flathead Lake. He returned to Canada later that summer, retired from the North West Company and died impoverished in Montreal in 1857, his works not finding a publisher until 1916. In spite of the primitive mapping methods available at the time, Thompson left a surprisingly detailed set of maps that chart from northwest Montana to the Pacific Coast.

Indians and individual trappers brought their furs to the trading posts, but the North West Company did not depend entirely on the posts to maintain trade. They organized large brigades, which were expeditions under experienced leaders to go out from the established posts and trap for furs. Donald McKenzie was chosen as the supervisor of the entire interior trade for the North West Company. He took charge of some of the brigades himself and extensively explored the Snake River in Idaho and even ranged through parts of the Yellowstone National Park area in Montana and Wyoming.

Competition between the North West Company and the Hudson's Bay Company was so fierce that it was called war—the Pemmican War. Each company raced to the field in the spring to get a head start on the other. Competition flourished for trade with a particular band of Indians, and each company was trying to outdo the other with gifts and other offerings. Prime trapping ground was also fiercely fought over, and violence often resulted.

Violence existed between the two British companies to such an extent that the threat from each other rivaled the threat from Indians. The peak of violence, called the Seven Oaks Massacre, occurred in 1816 in an episode on the Red River south of Lake Winnipeg at a small settlement called Fort Douglas, present-day Winnipeg, Manitoba. The Nor'Westers massacred a Hudson's Bay Company governor and twenty-one settlers at Hudson's Bay's Red River Colony.

Five years later, on March 26, 1821, the two companies merged, taking the name of the older company. Part of the consolidation agreement was that the "new" Company would hold the monopoly of trapping and trade in the previously disputed area for 21 years. The union was complete, and Hudson's Bay Company was still the largest and oldest commercial institution in North America.

Hudson's Bay Company

The Hudson's Bay Company was founded May 2, 1670, by charter from the British crown. The regal charter granted the Company absolute proprietorship,

Trade Goods and Hudson's Bay Blanket

Indians eagerly sought trade goods brought in by the trappers and traders, and would pay dearly for them. They were very willing to trade their furs for goods such as copper kettles, guns, powder and ball, knives, strike-a-lights, tomahawks, cloth, tobacco, beads, blankets, and such food items as sugar and coffee. Each item was worth so many "made beaver," or stretched and cured pelts, which originally was the Hudson's Bay Company term for the unit of exchange. For example, a trade gun might be worth twenty "made beaver," a skinning knife worth one, and a steel trap worth four.

The Hudson's Bay blankets were desirable trade items because they were durable and warm, and the colors appealed to Indians and trappers alike.

The red Hudson's Bay blanket was more popular than the common cream-colored blanket and, hence, worth more plews. Anyone wanting to call the trade items on the blanket his own would spend many beaver pelts.

According to Hudson's Bay Company records, the earliest mention of a Hudson's Bay "point" blanket is 1779. A company letter from 1780 states, "The 'Points' are known to every Indian as the price to be paid for the blanket, as two and a half 'Points'—two and a half beaver, three 'Points' three beaver…" The "points" (stripes up the side of one end) denoted the weight of the blanket, each point being a pound (a four-point blanket weighed four pounds). Various colors of blankets were made because the Indians liked the bright colors better than the standard cream color; there were seven standard colors in all.

The "point"-blanket coat was made popular by the French-Canadian *voyageurs*, or boatmen, and it is said they wore certain colors to denote where they came from. The Hudson's Bay blankets can still be purchased in the stores of Hudson's Bay Company, now known as "The Bay," as well as at other outlets. They are expensive and certainly do not reflect the value of a beaver pelt at today's prices.

supreme jurisdiction in all civil and military affairs, the power to make and interpret laws, and even the power to declare war against "pagan" peoples. The charter granted the Company access to all lands drained by the rivers that entered Hudson's Bay, called Rupert Land, and included territory in what is now Minnesota, North Dakota and Montana. The leaders literally had the power of life and death over employees and the people who lived within Hudson's Bay Company domain.

Based in London and with a major North American office in Montreal, "the Company," as it was known, had its eyes on western North America for the express purpose of obtaining furs. Consequently, western expansion was a main objective. Western expansion also meant southern expansion, which caused a few problems. Since the American-Canadian border was not defined as the 49th parallel east of the Rocky Mountains until 1818, and it was not until 1846 that that border was extended to the Pacific Ocean, both sides trapped as they pleased. A company laid claim to an area and did everything in its power to discourage intruders.

The Hudson's Bay Company was not bashful about extending its reach south. Several expeditions extensively explored the area of southern Montana and Idaho. The Hudson's Bay Company had its initials "HBC" on its property wherever it was located. Americans seeing these initials seemingly everywhere jokingly referred to the letters as meaning "Here Before Christ."

In the autumn of 1810, Hudson's Bay trader Joseph Howse built a small fur fort on the north end of Flathead Lake. (Nobody knows for sure where this post was located.) It was occupied through the winter of 1810-11 and abandoned in the spring. The purpose of the post was to counteract the presence of the North West Company in the Northwest. Howse House or Fort Howse has the distinction of being the only fort built by the Hudson's Bay Company west of the Rocky Mountains until consolidation with the North West Company in 1821.

In 1824 the Hudson's Bay Company built its Columbia Department headquarters on the Columbia River at Fort Vancouver (Washington) and named the shrewd Dr. John McLoughlin as governor. He sent brigades from Fort Vancouver and explored the northwest, reaching as far as western Montana. Trapping and trading continued for many years into the western reaches of Montana and Idaho; Hudson's Bay Company was reluctant to give up the rich trapping grounds.

Between 1811 and 1824 the Hudson's Bay Company kept an active presence in northwest Montana. What fur forts they operated largely have been forgotten. Writings from the period indicate that the Company always maintained a trading post in the area. Flathead Post (also called the second Salish House) was established in 1823 by Alexander Ross about five miles east of Thompson Falls.

February 10, 1824, Ross, who was charged with the lucrative Snake River trade, set out from Flathead Post near Thompson Falls for a winter trapping and exploring venture. His party consisted of 140 persons, some of whom were family members of the trappers, as well as a few Iroquois Indians hired to trap and to teach trapping techniques to the local natives.

Ross's journey took him to Hell Gate Valley near Missoula, up the Bitterroot River through the Bitterroot Valley, and on March 12 to Ross's Hole (which Ross called the Valley of Troubles) near Sula. Snow was deep; temperatures were near zero; and, passage east over the densely forested hills into the Big Hole Valley was next to impossible. For a few days, Ross waited for orders to turn back. When none came, amidst grumbling and near mutiny by his men, he started working his way east (via present-day Gibbons Pass) through ten-foot-high snowdrifts

Big Horn Canyon, now filled by water backed up by Yellowtail Dam at Fort Smith near Hardin, slices the Montana-Wyoming border. François Antoine Larocque of the North West Fur Company explored the canyon of the Big Horn River in 1805 and graphically recorded its spectacular rock formations and scenery. Today the National Park Service administers the two-state site from Fort Smith as the Big Horn Canyon National Recreation Area.

with the objective of reaching the Big Hole Valley. Men threatened to desert, so Ross promised to take the clothes of any persons caught deserting. The prospect of nudity in the spring mountains amidst those ten-foot snowdrifts changed all mutinous minds.

Tempers often ran high, but one month later, on April 14, after a fifteen-hour day of pandemonium, the group broke over the top into the Big Hole Valley. They remained in the Big Hole for twelve days enjoying the Boiling Spring at Jackson, where William Clark and nineteen of his men had camped in July of 1806.

Ross and his expedition trapped the Big Hole River and Willard's Creek—later to be known as Grasshopper Creek—and perhaps even at Bannack, the site of the first major gold strike in Montana in 1862. Ross then ventured into the Salmon River country via Lemhi Pass near Tendoy and Salmon, Idaho, and trapped that region extensively. In November of 1824 they returned to Flathead Post with the best return ever from a brigade's expedition and from the Snake River country—over 5,000 furs. When he returned, Ross was given command of Flathead Post, and Peter Skene Ogden replaced him as the head of the Snake River trade.

Between 1824 and 1830 Peter Skene Ogden led six forays into the immense drainages of the Snake River on behalf of the Hudson's Bay Company's Columbia Department. Reports abounded of the Snake River region being as rich a trapping field as could be found. In the years that followed, the Hudson's Bay Company increased its brigades in the field, adding James W. Dease and John Work as brigade leaders. The target was the fur-rich rivers and drainages of the Snake, Clark's Fork of the Columbia, and Missouri.

John Work, in charge of the Snake River brigade from 1831 until 1834, set out from Fort Nez Perce (Walla Walla) on September 11, 1831. His objective was trade with the Salish and Blackfeet Indians.

Pemmican and Jerky

One of the problems of the harsh life in the West was the preservation and transportation of food. Individual trappers or expeditions had to live off the land because they could not afford to pack the extra weight of heavy food. The dried staples, jerky and pemmican, served very well. Pemmican especially was nutritious since it contained not only meat and grease, but often berries. The word "pemmican" comes from two Cree words, *"pimii"* meaning fat, tallow or grease, and *"kaan,"* which means prepared. Pemmican was used by the Plains tribes long before the white explorers came. A North West Company trapper, Peter Pond, discovered its usefulness to trappers and introduced pemmican to white society.

Fellow Nor'Wester David Thompson gets the credit, however, for giving out the first recipe in Montana, probably about 1810 at the Salish House near Thompson Falls. Thompson writes of pemmican: "It is made of the lean and flesh parts of the bison, dried, smoked and pounded fine. In this state it is called 'beat meat.' The fat of the bison is of two qualities, called hard and soft. The former is from the inside of the animal, which when melted is called hard fat (properly grease), the latter is made from the large flakes of fat that lie on each side of the back bone, covering the ribs, which is readily separated, and when carefully melted resembles butter in softness and sweetness. Pemmican is made up in bags of ninety pounds weight, made of the parchment hide of the bison with the hair on. The proportion of pemmican when best made for keeping is twenty pounds of soft and the same of hard fat, slowly melted together, and at low warmth poured on fifty pounds of Beat Meat; well mixed together, and closely packed in a bag of thirty inches in length, by near twenty inches in breadth, and about four inches in thickness which makes them flat, the best shape for stowage and carriage." Sometimes it was seasoned with wild cherry, wild mint or chokecherries, pounded fine, stone and all.

Jerky, on the other hand, was much simpler. The meat of any animal was cut off in long thin strips about an inch or two wide and hung in the sun to dry. If salt brine was available the meat was soaked first, or even just salted, then hung to dry in the sun. Sometimes it was smoked first, adding to the flavor. Jerky was easily transportable and often kept in a pocket or parfleche bag for easy accessibility.

Bighorn Jerky

(One the many jerky recipes F.L. Graves has tried and enjoyed.)

$1^1/_2$ cups soy sauce
1 tablespoon lemon juice
$^1/_2$ cup stale beer
10 shakes tabasco
1 tablespoon liquid smoke
1 tablespoon honey
1 tablespoon dried mustard
$^1/_2$ tablespoon dried pepper
4 cloves pressed or finely chopped garlic
$1^1/_2$ pounds meat (wild or domestic—any will do), *all* fat and stringy gristle removed

Slice the meat into $^1/_8$- to $^1/_4$-inch-thick strips. Mix all ingredients well and marinate overnight. Dehydrate at 118°F, usually 12 to 16 hours, until dry but not brittle. Dry in oven at lowest setting if dehydrator not available.

With this enterprising group were various family members of trappers and traders, including Work's three small daughters and someone he called his "little Walla Walla Indian housekeeper" as baby-sitter. Like most other trapping expeditions, this one also included clerks and store-keepers who would look after such trading items as guns, beads, vermilion, axes, mirrors, knives, blankets, coffee, clay pipes and tobacco. Whenever the expedition encountered Indians with furs, these men would set up shop. Their take on some days understandably would be greater than what the trappers would bring in from the field.

Work and his party traveled east following the Clearwater River in part, over Lolo Pass, and ended up at Lolo Hot Springs, Montana, on October 13, 1831. Work reported many beaver taken, as well as deer, elk, bear and sheep. The party met the Bitterroot River (named for the flower that grows in profusion on its banks) near the present town of Lolo and followed it to Hell Gate Valley (Missoula) where they spent the night of October 20. Ten days later, just west of Ovando near Monture Creek, Work lamented in his journal: "Some marks of the Americans are seen. The Indians [with him] had hunted the little forks up this far, and probably all above this is hunted by Americans, so that nothing is left for us."

Within several weeks of leaving Hell Gate Valley, Work lost several of his men to Blackfeet attacks. From Hell Gate he had moved to trap the area of Deer Lodge, Divide, and the Beaverhead Valley. Thursday, November 17, 1831, he noted the Beaverhead Rock south of Dillon, which had been mentioned by Lewis and Clark on August 10, 1805. Work also noted immense herds of buffalo in the area, and how fat they were.

He and his group journeyed via Shoshone Cove, or Horse Prairie, to the Salmon River country, spending nearly a month trapping. January 4, 1832, he reen-

tered Montana and trapped the Beaverhead Valley once more from Red Rock near Clark Canyon Dam to the Point of Rocks near Twin Bridges. He especially liked the Beaverhead because of the abundance of buffalo for food, and the wide open spaces in which he could spot Blackfeet or other bands of Indians.

From January 28 until February 3, 1832, John Work's expedition was camped about ten miles north of Dillon, about where the railroad terminus Apex is now located. He remained in camp longer than was usual because the sick and wounded were unable to move and the weather was inclement. On Monday, January 30, the group was attacked at daybreak by a party of at least 300 Piegans (Blackfeet) and Gros Ventres. The attack lasted until noon, Work's group sustaining one Flathead killed and eight wounded. Work's arm was slightly injured and his "Walla Walla Indian housekeeper dangerously wounded." He recorded in his journal, "A brisk fire was kept up on both sides until noon, at one time they had surrounded our camp, but kept a considerable distance." The cannon Work had with him burst on the third discharge, and was presumably left, becoming the object of searches years later. Work and his party left Montana via Horse Prairie and Bannack Pass the second week of March, encountering many other adventures along the way. His exciting expedition was not unlike others to the fur beds of the West; only the locations differed.

Trapping generally was productive in spite of the harassment by the Blackfeet Indians. The number of animal pelts grew steadily until 1837, when one source lists the Hudson's Bay Company's harvest at 26,735 pelts. Then, the number of beaver in the region steadily declined because of the heavy trapping pressure. In spite of many areas being trapped out, exciting trapping forays continued.

The Americans were invading the region in greater numbers and were claiming the territory as their own with greater

Above: Beaver nibbling on alder twigs.

Below: Beaver dam and pond. Beaver will dam a stream to make a pond in which to continue their activities.

frequency and enthusiasm. In the Flathead country, vigorous measures were taken to overcome American aggressiveness. Flathead Post was moved farther east to ward off American ventures and ultimately was moved to Post Creek near Ronan and Charlo and renamed Fort Connah. In 1847, Angus McDonald completed construction of Fort Connah, which has the distinction of being the last Hudson's Bay Company post to be constructed in what is now the United States. In 1871 Fort Connah was closed by Duncan McDonald, son of old Angus who had opened it twenty-five years before.

The day of the beaver-fur trade had begun to close in western Montana by the early 1850s. Many Indians and whites continued to hunt and trap furs and sell or trade them at such places as Fort Owen in the Bitterroot near Stevensville or Fort Connah. Silk had replaced beaver in its value for hats, and buffalo had become the fur of choice. The days of the romantic fur trade were over.

The Importance of Beaver

The felt hat came into greater prominence in the early 1800s. Fur coats and scarves were in fashion and were warm. Europe set the fashion trends of the day, and her cold, damp climate dictated a lot of the styles of the so-called civilized world. Beaver fur was popular because of its natural felting. The rich underfur, called *muffoon*, is microscopically barbed and "felts up" better than any other fur. Felt is natural, without any adhesives or weaving, and depends on the matting quality of its fibers. While the beaver-fur hat was in vogue in Europe and North America, the price of beaver was up and free enterprise was aimed toward its procurement. A continent would be explored; free enterprise moved ahead full bore on an international scale; and, an entirely new, major chapter in American and Canadian history had begun.

Beaver Prices

1800	$1.00 per pound at St. Louis
1809	$2.00 per pound at St. Louis
1811	$4.00 per pound at St. Louis
1812-1815	$1.50 per pound, and rose steadily
1825	$3.00 per pound at St. Louis
1834	Kenneth McKenzie paid more than $4 per pound at Fort Union
1840	Decline of prices
1848	$1.00 for a large skin at Fort Vancouver
Today	$25 to $35 per skin

Buffalo

The American Fur Company paid $4.50 for a first-class robe from 1820 to 1840.

American Fur Companies

Lisa, Menard, Morrison and Company

Lisa, Menard, Morrison and Company was the first American trapping effort into Montana and the Northwest. This group seems to have had no formal name and little formal organization. Manuel Lisa, who became excited by the reports of the vast numbers of natural resources noted by the Lewis and Clark Expedition, was the primary organizer. Lisa's expedition left St. Louis in the spring of 1807 with the purpose of establishing posts among Indians of the Upper Missouri who, for the most part, had been "untouched" by American traders. A keelboat carried items for barter, and progress was limited to the slow rate at which the boat could be cordelled upstream.

With Lisa was his right-hand man, George Drouillard, formerly a hunter and interpreter for the Lewis and Clark Expedition. Near the mouth of the Platte River, not too far from present-day Omaha, the expedition encountered a solitary white man canoeing downriver. Lisa knew the man—John Colter, another former member of the Lewis and Clark Expedition. Colter was persuaded to turn around and join the expedition, which was the best luck Lisa could have had. Colter had been to the regions of the Upper Missouri where they were heading, and his knowledge of the area and expertise were extensive. At the junction of the Missouri and Yellowstone rivers, they decided to go up the Yellowstone and ended up at the mouth of the Big Horn River near Hysham in November 1807. At this juncture, they were in the heart of Crow country. They built Fort Manuel Lisa, also called Fort Raymond (named for Lisa's son Remon). According to Lisa's journals, Fort Manual Lisa was constructed "on the wooded point between the two rivers just above their conjunction." Temporary living shelters were hastily constructed, and the construction of the fort began. Fort Manuel Lisa was the first permanent white settlement in Montana.

Manuel Lisa sent John Colter out on a winter odyssey to make contact with the Crows, to advertise the trading post at the mouth of the Big Horn River, and to induce the Indians to come and trade. Colter's solo and circuitous journey took him via Pryor Gap to Yellowstone Park and into Jackson Hole country. He finally located a large camp of about 1,000 Crow Indians near Cody, Wyoming. With his mission completed, he started back for Fort Manuel Lisa. Colter is thought to be the first white man to see the natural wonders of Yellowstone National Park. At the fort, the stories he told of the Yellowstone with its geysers and boiling-mud paint pots branded him a champion liar and the region he visited as "Colter's Hell."

The men trapped the spring and summer season from Fort Manuel Lisa, and many Indians brought furs to the fort to trade. Late in the summer of 1808, Lisa returned to St. Louis with the furs and tales he had acquired, leaving his men to further his aims in the Upper Missouri. A few of the men journeyed to the Three Forks of the Missouri to trap the rich fur grounds near present-day Three Forks. The Blackfeet were not happy with the white intrusion. In the opinion of the whites, hostile relations with the Blackfeet often were traced to the Lewis and Clark Expedition and a fight in which two Blackfeet were killed. (Historians later determined that the Indians involved were Gros Ventre.)

One of the most famous tales to emerge from the fur-trade era, and even the West, occurred in the fall of 1808. John Colter and John Potts were trapping the Jefferson River together. They were jumped and captured by Blackfeet, and in the beginning minutes of the encounter Potts was killed. Colter was stripped naked and told to run for his life. And run he did, barefoot, over prickly-pear cactus and the rocky ground. He looked back and was surprised to discover that he had outdistanced all but one pursuer, a warrior with a spear, who was gaining on him. He turned suddenly, startling the Indian, who lost his balance. Colter seized the spear, pinned the Indian to the ground with it, and took off again to the Madison River. He dived into the river and secreted himself in a pile of driftwood, where he remained to elude the horde of angry Blackfeet. When night came, Colter swan downstream and went ashore. Seven days later, still naked and barefoot, starving, and with his feet full of cactus spikes and slivers, he reached Fort Manuel Lisa on the Big Horn, a distance of over 250 miles. The "champion liar" had another story to tell.

The War of 1812

The War of 1812 between the United States and Great Britain was significant to the fur trade. Intense rivalry existed between the Americans and the British, each vying for superiority. The war led to the surrender of Fort Astoria to the British, ending Astor's efforts on the northwest coast. The British members of Astoria's Pacific Fur Company refused to fight their countrymen and surrendered Astoria to the British. Most of the British employees of Astor deserted the Americans and went to the employ of the North West Company, among them Alexander Ross.

The effect of the War of 1812 was to curtail the volume of furs obtained, for two basic reasons. Since Astoria had been surrendered, the American trappers' diminished territory was essentially east of the Rockies. Second, the war stopped the export of beaver and forced a decline in prices. Consequently, the trade with the Indians declined because the furs were not worth as much. American relations with the various Indian tribes declined, which, of course, was encouraged by the British to their great advantage.

The Missouri Fur Company was practically driven from the field. When the partners of the Missouri Fur Company left St. Louis in May of 1812, they took only two boats, loaded with $11,000 worth of merchandise. With the threat of war with the British, the men in charge did not want to risk more. Primary partner in the Missouri Fur Company and field captain Manuel Lisa is given the credit for keeping the Sioux from joining the British in the War of 1812. Lisa treated the Indians fairly, primarily the Sioux, and earned their respect and friendship and gave them lavish gifts.

Sacrifice Cliff above the Yellowstone River near Billings.

Missouri Fur Company

When Manuel Lisa returned to St. Louis in the fall of 1808, he organized the Missouri Fur Company. Among the primary officers were Manuel Lisa, Pierre Menard, Pierre Chouteau, Jr., Auguste Chouteau, Jr., Reuben Lewis (brother of Meriwether Lewis), William Clark and Andrew Henry. When spring of 1809 arrived, Lisa wasted no time leaving for the rich fur grounds of the Yellowstone. His group began the return to Fort Manuel Lisa as early as ice breakup on the rivers would allow, taking much of the summer for the arduous trip and establishing trading posts among various tribes along the way. Lisa and his party of nearly 300 men arrived at the little fort at the mouth of the Big Horn near Hysham in late October 1809. They spent the winter at Fort Manuel Lisa since it was too late in the season to go on to the Three Forks and establish a post there.

As soon as weather permitted in the

spring of 1810, a group guided by John Colter consisting of, among others, Andrew Henry, Reuben Lewis, George Drouillard and Pierre Menard went up the Yellowstone, over Bozeman Pass to the Three Forks of the Missouri. On April 3, 1810, they began to construct Three Forks Post (also called Fort Henry) on a neck of land between the Jefferson and Madison rivers about two miles above the rivers' confluence. The post was about 300 feet square and consisted of a double stockade of cottonwood logs. Trapping brigades had been sent out from the day of the group's arrival, and hopes were high that over 300 packs of beaver (at 100 pelts per pack) would be taken the first year from the virgin country. Success was short-lived. Between the unfriendliness of the Blackfeet and the friendliness of the grizzly bears, the stress level of the trappers was at a record level.

On April 10, one week to the day after construction of Three Forks Post began, tragedy struck that undermined morale and ultimately led to the closure of the post and abandonment of the area. George Drouillard, certainly no stranger to the dangers of the area, became careless and began trapping by himself. He was trapping on the Jefferson with two Delaware Indian trappers nearby when they were jumped by Blackfeet and killed. When Drouillard and the two Indian trappers failed to return, a search party went out and found the bodies within hearing distance of help. But, due to the prevailing winds, nothing had been heard. April 12, just two days after the death of Drouillard, five more trappers were killed by Blackfeet, and their traps, guns, pelts and horses were taken. Interestingly enough, the traps and pelts later turned up in British hands. In the fall, the decision was made to abandon the post and relocate.

Andrew Henry decided to go up the Madison, cross over the Divide and establish a post, Henry's Post, on the North

The interior of a trading house. LEE KAISER

Fork (now called Henry's Fork) of the Snake River in Idaho. This was the first American fort west of the Rocky Mountains. Henry's Post and Fort Manuel Lisa did not survive long. By the next summer, the Missouri Fur Company had withdrawn all posts from above the Mandan villages in North Dakota. The War of 1812 had dampened trapping in the West as the price of beaver fell below a profitable margin. The company abandoned its efforts for the time being, Manuel Lisa building Fort Lisa at modern Council Bluffs, Iowa, and concentrating efforts in that area.

In 1819, the Missouri Fur Company was reorganized. At the helm was Manuel

Free Trappers

The "free trapper" is certainly one of the more romantic characters to evolve in the West. He roamed the Rocky Mountains at will, dictated by his knowledge of the area and his good sense. He owed allegiance to no one—not a company or a family. Sometimes he traveled alone; sometimes he had companions for company or protection, but generally never more than one or two close friends. His furs were sold to the highest bidder, often at a rendezvous to avoid the "civilization" of a fur fort.

Most of the men considered free trappers were unattached for periods during their trapping careers and were signed on with a company at other times. Jim Bridger was one who periodically signed on with a company and then would quit to try his luck on his own or with some friends. Kit Carson was considered a free trapper as well; he spent much of his time in the mountains on the Upper Missouri. Although more famous for his exploits in the southwest, Carson did trap the Three Forks and Beaverhead rivers, and the Yellowstone and its drainages. Old Bill Williams began his career as an itinerant preacher in Missouri. He got tired of that lifestyle and headed west to the mountains; he called the Clark's Fork of the Snake River home. Williams often would disappear for months at a time, then appear at a rendezvous or a trading post fresh in from his secret trapping grounds with his packs full. He would trade and generally spend all of his earnings, then make for the mountains to begin the cycle again. He was killed by Indians in about 1832, the fate of quite a few free trappers.

The free trapper fiercely guarded and cherished his independence, often recognizing his own antisocial nature. By the 1830s, there were probably several hundred free trappers in the Rocky Mountains. The beaver trade dwindled in the 1840s; the last rendezvous was held in 1840. The free trapper was becoming a thing of the past. His way of life now exists only in books and in the hearts and minds of those longing to live the free but dangerous lifestyle. On the average, one trapper was killed in the Rocky Mountains every ten days. Many of these were free trappers caught alone by Indians. Where they perished, no one will ever know...they just disappeared, never to be heard from again.

Lisa; there were eight other partners, none of whom was a member of the original company. Among the eight were Joshua Pilcher, Moses Carson, Andrew Woods, Andrew Drips and Robert Jones. In the fall of 1821, Joshua Pilcher returned to the mouth of the Big Horn on the south side of the Yellowstone and rebuilt the company post about where Fort Manuel Lisa was previously located near Hysham. The new fort was named Fort Benton (not to be confused with Fort Benton of the American Fur Company on the Missouri River) in honor of Missouri senator Thomas Hart Benton, a supporter in Congress of the fur trade. Reestablishment of trade with the Crows was important, and the Big Horn was the heart of Crow country. Also, Fort Benton on the Yellowstone would be a good jumping-off place to establish trade with the Blackfeet, still a priority in the eyes of the fur-company managers.

Late in the fall of 1822, an expedition of 180 men under the leadership of Robert Jones and Michael Immel arrived at Fort Benton on the Yellowstone to spend the winter. Early in the spring of 1823 they set out for the Three Forks area and found that during the preceding ten years the Blackfeet had trapped it out. Disappointed, they returned to the Yellowstone, thinking Crow country would be a bit safer and more productive. The small group was spotted by a war party of 400 Blackfeet. Jones and Immel had made the mistake of not having flankers out to see if they were being followed. As the two separate parties neared the mouth of Alkali Creek near Billings on May 31, 1823, the Blackfeet planned their attack. They decided to go around the trappers and ambush them from above on the cliffs as the unsuspecting party climbed a narrow trail. As the trappers were well up the ascending trail, the Blackfeet attacked, killing Michael Immel almost immediately. Robert Jones tried to rally his men, but was cut to pieces. All in all, the Jones-Im-

mel Massacre saw seven trappers killed and four wounded, and nearly all their property lost including 35 packs of beaver, horses, and guns—totaling $15,000 in 1823 prices. Later that day, the survivors reached the comparative safety of a Crow camp at the mouth of Pryor Creek near Huntley. This disaster led Pilcher to withdraw his trappers from the Upper Missouri entirely. The Missouri Fur Company finally folded in 1830.

Some modern historians attribute the Blackfeet hostilities, in large part, to the British. Most of the firearms the Indians used in attacks on the Americans came from British territory and were paid for in part by pelts stolen in raids on the Americans or trapped by traps stolen in those same raids.

Rocky Mountain Fur Company

The Rocky Mountain Fur Company was not *formally* organized until 1830 when Jedediah Smith, David E. Jackson and William Sublette sold the company to five seasoned trappers. In the spring of 1822, however, William H. Ashley and Andrew Henry advertised for one hundred "enterprising young men" to ascend the Missouri River to trap for up to three years. Answering the call were men such as Jedediah Smith, David Jackson, Milton and William Sublette, James Bridger, Thomas Fitzpatrick, Hugh Glass and Mike Fink. Both Henry and Ashley had worked for the Missouri Fur Company during its peak and had applied the successes and failures of their previous experience to their new venture.

Their designs for the new company included three innovative and ultimately successful concepts. First, this would be the only American fur company devoted exclusively to trapping. Prior to this time, a major emphasis of the companies also was trading. Trading included cultivating the Indians' friendship with various ex-

The Madison River at its junction with the Jefferson River is where the Three Forks Post was built in 1810. This area saw the killing of John Potts and John Colter's race for his life.

LEE KAISER

Left: *A trapper scrapes flesh from a newly acquired beaver pelt to ready it for packing.*
Below: *Alkali Creek at Billings, Montana, the site of the Jones-Immel Massacre in 1823. This attack destroyed the enterprising spirit of the Missouri Fur Company.*

F. LEE GRAVES

Rendezvous

Andrew Henry and William Ashley of the Rocky Mountain Fur Company get the credit for the creation of the rendezvous system. The partners were seeking a way to keep their men in the mountains trapping instead of having to come back to a trading post or even go to St. Louis periodically to unload their furs and replenish their supplies. Such an arrangement would suit the mountain men just fine, for most did not want to return to civilization anyway, even for a short time. Since the Henry-Ashley men were trapping their own furs, they would not need a trading post as a central location. In order to dispose of their furs and to replenish their supplies, the trappers needed a place to meet. The meeting place was called a rendezvous, coined from Middle French meaning "present yourselves."

On November 3, 1824, Ashley left Fort Atkinson, Nebraska (fourteen miles north of Omaha) guiding a pack train loaded with supplies for his men. His goal was the central Rockies, there to meet his men in the spring. The site selected was in southern Wyoming on the Henry's Fork about twenty miles from its confluence with the Green River. Ashley recorded that there were 129 men present at the Rendezvous of 1825, including 29 Hudson's Bay Company deserters. One hundred packs of furs with a total value of nearly $50,000 went from the site to St. Louis that fall. The rendezvous was a huge success, and plans were made for the next one.

Rendezvous were held on a yearly basis at various locations until 1840, mainly in Wyoming, but Pierre's Hole in Idaho and Bear Lake in northwest Utah were favorite sites as well.

Whites and Indians alike enjoyed the rendezvous. Company men, opposition fur traders (even the British), free trappers, and Indians and their families all looked forward to the festive gathering, the primary business venture in the mountains. "Moccasin telegraph" (word of mouth) advertised the event. People appeared long before the date chosen to start trading, not wanting to miss out on any of the fun.

Mountain men could trade for the latest in rifles just brought from a maker such as Hawken, a Green River knife, tobacco, sugar and other staples to make life easier. Everyone eagerly participated in the shooting matches, wrestling matches, knife-throwing contests and other feats of skill. Storytelling and general socializing went on day and night. Trading "shops" were the backs of wagons, blankets on the ground, or trading was simply one-on-one. Everything had its price, which most often was attained.

After the rendezvous the mountain man returned to the mountains with goods needed for another year of trapping, often with new partners, both male and female. Some even returned with nothing except their basic gear, either having lost their furs gambling or having spent them on women and whiskey.

The rendezvous system lasted until 1840 when it was no longer practical to take goods to the mountains in such quantity to trade. That last year, 1840, the rendezvous was held at Green River in Wyoming. Father Pierre-Jean DeSmet was in attendance and spent four days resting at the site on his way farther west. His

Left: *A modern "rendezvouer" clad in skins enjoys the light rain.*
Below: *Racing was a favorite pastime at a rendezvous.*

descriptions are interesting, particularly one noting a Snake Indian expedition to attack the Blackfeet.

But the market was simply not there anymore, and one seasoned rendezvouser and trapper even remarked that the rendezvous was dull. LeRoy Hafen sums up the feeling in his book, *Broken Hand*: "This was the last fur-trade rendezvous [1840], the finale to those spectacular mountain assemblages that for sixteen years had been the outstanding annual event, the unique institution of the Rocky Mountain West. To the grizzled trappers who had seen the rise and fall of the beaver skin business, this final gathering brought bewilderment and regret."

Jim Bridger.
MONTANA HISTORICAL SOCIETY

outright and was free to do with them as he wished.

Eighteen-year-old Jim Bridger got his start in the mountains in this way, being "grubstaked" by Ashley. This incentive program worked well; it gave the individual trapper a direct profit from his work, which in turn greatly increased profits to the company. In 1822 the demand for pelts was great, with prime pelts going for $3.50 to $4.00 per pound. Beaver was available on the Lower Missouri, below the mouth of the Big Sioux River near Sioux City, Iowa, but beaver on the Upper Missouri had thicker and richer coats and commanded a higher price. Therefore, the profiteers had their sights set on the Upper Missouri.

The partners agreed that William Ashley would remain in St. Louis and handle the management and politics of the company. Andrew Henry, on the other hand, had little "business sense" and was often in debtor's court for one reason or another, but was a master in the mountains. To him fell the task of leading the expeditions, building trading posts, directing trapping forays and seeing that the furs obtained reached market safely. Each leader was accomplished in his field and complemented the other well.

In 1822 Andrew Henry led the first Rocky Mountain Fur Company expedition, which ascended the Missouri River to the mouth of the Yellowstone River, where a temporary post, Fort Henry, was erected. With this expedition was Jim Bridger, on his first of many forays into the mountains. During the spring of 1823 Henry explored and trapped the Missouri and many of its drainages with success. But his losses were heavy as well—such as on May 4, 1823, when the Blackfeet jumped Henry's party of eleven men near the mouth of the Smith River between Ulm and Great Falls. Four men were killed. Thirty traps had to be abandoned in the river and 172 others buried. Henry returned with low spirits to Fort Henry,

pensive gifts, often with little or no immediate return on the investment.

Second, the trappers would work out of a trading post, more accurately called a fur fort, which would be used as a base of operations. The trappers would trap the furs and take them to their home base to turn in and receive credit. Beginning in 1825, the rendezvous served the purpose. The company saw to it that the furs were shipped back to St. Louis; the trapper himself did not have to worry about that at all.

Third, the trappers would work for the company as independent contractors. When a trapper signed on with Ashley-Henry, he received a gun, powder, lead and other supplies he needed in exchange for half the furs obtained. The other half of the furs the trapper owned where several of his men decided to return to St. Louis, having had enough of risky mountain life to suit them.

Henry decided to relocate farther upriver because adverse pressure from the Mandans and Arikaras at Fort Henry kept his men constantly on guard with a high level of stress; and, he found Fort Henry too far from prime beaver grounds up the Yellowstone River. During the summer of 1823 he erected the Big Horn Post near Hysham at the mouth of the Big Horn River, near the site where Fort Manuel Lisa had been constructed 16 years before.By the fall of 1823 the Rocky Mountain Fur Company was the only fur company on the Missouri River; the Missouri Fur Company had abandoned the field after the Jones-Immel Massacre that spring. Was the great risk worth it? Henry thought so, and decided to continue in spite of the fact that, on the average, one trapper was killed every ten days in fur country. The group spent the winter of 1823-24 at the little fort at the mouth of the Big Horn doing some trading with the Crows and subsisting on buffalo, deer and elk the hunters provided them. The long days found Henry and his men around the campfires telling stories, mending equipment, smoking pipes, and otherwise passing time. They began their successful spring hunt as soon as ice was off the rivers and streams. However, a letter from Henry to a friend (which is now in the archives of the Missouri Historical Society in St. Louis) states, "A fortune could be made if it were not for the difficulty of the Indians." In August 1824 Andrew Henry returned to St. Louis, never to return to the mountains.

William Ashley managed the field op-

The Cache

One of the problems the trappers faced when they were in a hurry to leave for one reason or another was what to do with their furs and extra goods. They devised a relatively safe and sure temporary storage that, if made well enough, was safe from the elements and even from discovery by rival trappers or Indians. The device was the "cache" (pronounced *cash*), which was a hole dug straight down for about six to twelve inches, then gradually widened in the shape of a cone. The amount of goods to be cached determined the size. Some were made large enough for a man to crawl into. If the cache was to be left for a longer period of time, the inside was lined with rocks, sticks, or even a buffalo or elk hide to keep out moisture. In a well-made cache, the merchandise inside would be safe for years. It is a sure bet that trappers' caches lie undiscovered in the Rocky Mountains to this day, full of furs, trade goods and who knows what all.

Above: Crow Indian graves near Pryor, Montana.
Left: Muddy Creek area in Big Horn County between St. Xavier and Pryor. This part of Montana was extensively explored by Nor'wester François Antoine Larocque in 1805.

Facing page, top: Fragile prickly pear (Opuntia fragilis) *is common to the West. Spines from this cactus were picked from the feet of John Colter at Fort Manuel Lisa following his harrowing escape from Blackfeet in the fall of 1808.*

erations himself in 1824 and 1825. His plan for constructing a series of fur posts on the Missouri River was abandoned. He decided to try a new method of obtaining furs, which he called the "rendezvous system." The rendezvous was to be a yearly gathering of trappers, traders, and Indians at a predetermined location for the purpose of turning over furs for supplies needed for another year in the mountains. He decided to hold the first rendezvous (1825) twenty miles up the Henry's Fork from its confluence with the Green River in southern Wyoming. The concept was used successfully until 1840.

In 1826 Ashley retired from the fur trade, returning to Missouri, where he was elected to Congress. He sold the Rocky Mountain Fur Company to Jedediah Smith, David Jackson and William Sublette. During the four years Smith, Jackson and Sublette owned the company, they spent every available minute in the field obtaining furs. Most of their time, however, was spent trapping the rivers and streams of Utah, Idaho and Wyoming, with an occasional expedition into Montana and the Southwest. Trapping was generally good, with the partners turning a nice profit. For example, reports indicate in 1827 they realized a nice profit of $22,690, good by anybody's standards. The next year was even better—over 7,000 pounds of beaver and a few other skins brought nearly $36,000 at the St. Louis market.

In 1828 David Jackson and Thomas Fitzpatrick trapped the Flathead region of northwest Montana. They found the Hudson's Bay Company entrenched in the area, which helped neither their spirits nor the trapping. Hudson's Bay reports even made mention that the American expedition had to trade some of their small cache of furs to them for necessary supplies. Pickin's were slim.

Early in 1829 Robert Campbell led a small expedition—31 men—from the Flat-head region to southeastern Montana and northern Wyoming to trap and trade with the Crows. With him was Jim Beckwourth, a husky black man who, according to George Laycock in *The Mountain Men*, came to the mountains after thumping the head of the blacksmith to whom he was apprenticed and taking "unauthorized leave." Beckwourth gained fame in the mountains by, among other things, being adopted into the Crow tribe as one of their chiefs.

By 1830, Smith, Jackson and William Sublette had amassed a small fortune and decided to get out of the business "while they still had their hair." On August 4, at the rendezvous of 1830 held near Riverton, Wyoming, the three partners sold their firm to Henry Fraeb, Jean Baptiste Gervais, James Bridger, Thomas Fitzpatrick and Milton Sublette. The three sellers returned to St. Louis with over $75,000 in furs and they retired wealthy men.

Since the season was late, the new owners headed toward their wintering sites, trapping along the way. Fraeb and Gervais, along with 32 trappers and families, headed for the Snake River country of Idaho and Utah and probably wintered in Cache Valley, near Logan, Utah. The company's major wintering site that year, however, was at the mouth of the Powder River about seven miles west of present-day Terry, Montana. Accounts vary, but between 80 and 200 people wintered there, including Jim Bridger, Tom Fitzpatrick and Milton Sublette. (The discrepancy in the total number perhaps is that 80 trappers are counted and the total of 200 includes families.)

For the next two years, the Rocky Mountain Fur Company dispatched its main body of trappers to the Blackfeet country of Montana and, to some extent, the Flathead. They wintered on the Salmon River and crossed over into the Flathead Lake area to trap, in some cases alongside the already established Hud-

Fur Country Celebrities

Fort Union had its share of famous visitors during the years. Most visitors ventured farther upriver on both the Yellowstone and Missouri rivers. They contributed immensely to our understanding of the period and of the trade itself, because often they left comprehensive journals and artistic renditions of the area, its people and events. The Swiss writer and artist Rudolf Friederich Kurz recorded six years of his life (1846 to 1852) on the Mississippi and Upper Missouri in a journal and in many drawings and paintings. Kurz lived at Fort Union in 1851 and 1852; his narratives are candid and descriptive.

In 1833 German nobleman Maximilian, Prince of Wied, collected geological specimens and plants, which added to our knowledge of botany and geology; he also left a journal. With Maximilian was Karl Bodmer, an artist who left detailed paintings and drawings of Fort Union, Fort McKenzie and other places they visited. Bodmer Point northeast of Fort Union is named for the location from which he painted Fort Union and the surrounding area.

Pierre-Jean DeSmet.

In 1843, sixty-year-old naturalist and painter John James Audubon and four other men visited Fort Union and Montana collecting bird and animal specimens. Out of this party came no fewer than three diaries, several letters, and two paintings of Fort Union, then in its fourteenth year.

George Catlin visited the Upper Missouri in 1832 aboard the steamer *Yellow Stone* and left elaborate, often romantic, views of life on the prairie. Pierre-Jean DeSmet, S.J., made the first of his many visits to Fort Union in 1840 and left several written accounts of his visits. Fellow Roman Catholic priest, Father Nicholas Point, did intricate pencil sketches, which recorded meticulous impressions of Indians, forts, and locations he visited.

son's Bay men. From the Hudson's Bay Company's Flathead Post, chief factor Francis Ermatinger wrote his brother in the spring of 1833, "The Americans have reaped the harvest, and all I can expect is part of the gleanings." The ubiquitous Americans were slowly but surely enticing the Flathead Indian trade away from the British.

The rich beaver streams of the Missouri drainages such as Beaverhead, Madison, Jefferson and Gallatin were trapped again with great success. The Rocky Mountain Fur Company was doing such a good business in the beaver trade that the rival American Fur Company was following some of their brigade expeditions into Montana, Idaho and Wyoming to learn the secrets of their success and

their trapping grounds. When the Rocky Mountain trappers arrived at the 1832 rendezvous at Pierre's Hole just west of the Tetons in Wyoming, they found the rivals already there cashing in on the furs. Henry Vanderburgh and Andrew Drips were particularly pesky and very willing to tag along to learn of Rocky Mountain Fur Company secret trapping grounds and methods.

The Blackfeet Indians still were posing a challenge to all white trappers, but especially resented the Rocky Mountain Fur Company; they believed the company was not only plundering their fur beds, but also supplying their enemies—Crows, Salish and Nez Perce—with guns. Kit Carson, a member of Jim Bridger's brigade in 1834, was quoted as saying, "A trapper

Confluence of the Yellowstone and Missouri rivers, western North Dakota. This area saw several fur and military forts in the 1800s.

F. LEE GRAVES

Right: A spring day along the Missouri River in Lewis and Clark County north of Wolf Creek Canyon. The verdant hills are home to game that was the source of food, clothing and shelter to the Indians and trappers.

Below: Lewis and Clark Festival, Great Falls, Montana. A dugout canoe was one of the most popular methods of transportation on the waterways of the West in the 1800s. This dugout is a replica hand-hewn from a cottonwood tree.

Andrew Dawson of the
American Fur Company.
MONTANA HISTORICAL SOCIETY

near Granger in southwestern Wyoming, the partners of the Rocky Mountain Fur Company agreed to dissolve. Fraeb and Gervais sold out for next to nothing. Bridger, Fitzpatrick and Milton Sublette merged with Fontenelle and Drips to form a new fur company. The days of the Rocky Mountain Fur Company were over, after twelve great years. That period saw the frontier schooling of Kit Carson, Jim Bridger, Thomas Fitzpatrick and provided the bases of stories, both fact and fiction, for years to come.

American Fur Company

The American Fur Company was to the Americans what the Hudson's Bay Company was to the British. It represented a major effort by big money with government support to monopolize a lucrative enterprise, in this case, the fur trade. The American Fur Company was formed in New York in 1808 by John Jacob Astor and was the longest-lived American fur company, lasting until the Civil War. Astor's vision of his fur empire was global, not just confined to North America. At first his base of operations was at Mackinac, Michigan, and was called the Northern Department. Then, in 1822 the American Fur Company established a Western Department based in St. Louis. In 1827, Astor absorbed the Pacific Fur Company based in Astoria, Oregon, which saw his dream expand from coast to coast, except for a big void consisting of the Rocky Mountains. It did not take him long to fill in the gap, especially with Pierre Chouteau, Jr. now in charge of the Western Department.

Also in 1827, the Upper Missouri Outfit was created to expand the robe and fur trade to the vast expanse above the Big Sioux River, referred to as the Upper Missouri. Kenneth McKenzie was in charge of this operation and was a competent manager. In 1829 McKenzie founded Fort

could hardly go a mile without being fired upon."
One of the effects of the Rocky Mountain Fur Company, especially under Smith, Jackson and Sublette, was to inspire rivals in the fur business. The greatest of these rivals was the American Fur Company, which was the primary cause of the Rocky Mountain Fur Company's demise. Rocky Mountain did not have the financial base to compete with the American Fur Company. The American Fur Company fixed prices of beaver and goods sent to the mountains. The Rocky Mountain Company could not compete with selling beaver at low prices and paying trappers high wages, $1,500 in 1834. Finally, on June 20, 1834, at the rendezvous on Ham's Fork

Union near the junction of the Missouri and Yellowstone rivers on the Montana-North Dakota border. The Missouri River was the "moving road" to and from the West.

The confluence of the Missouri and Yellowstone rivers long had been a prime location for fur-trading activities. Several temporary posts had been erected prior to and since Fort Union was founded in 1829. The location was the natural jumping-off place for the two prime beaver streams, the Missouri and Yellowstone rivers and their tributaries. Above Fort Union the Yellowstone was the primary way to the Crows, and the Missouri the way to the Blackfeet. James Kipp was most likely in charge of building Fort Union. The bourgeois, or manager, of the fort was Kenneth McKenzie. A 220-foot by 240-foot palisade of vertical cottonwood logs was constructed on the north bank of the Missouri. Naturally, the main gate faced the river, and on the northeast and southwest corners stood two-story stone bastions protecting opposite sides of the fort.

Kenneth McKenzie decided to work on the Blackfeet trade first, and in the late spring of 1831 he sent James Kipp and 44 men in a keelboat up the Missouri River near the mouth of the Marias River near Loma. On the north bank of the Missouri River, Kipp built a temporary post called Fort Piegan for the subtribe of the Blackfoot Confederacy native to the area. Fort Piegan was only 110 feet square and supported a 25-foot-high palisade with three large buildings. Kipp purposely offered the Blackfeet much higher prices for furs than the Hudson's Bay traders were offering, and trade commenced at once. Reports state business was so good that the traders acquired over 2,000 furs during the first ten days of trade.

Not all tribes of the Blackfoot Confederacy, however, were friendly. The Bloods, or Kainai, put Fort Piegan under siege for a period of two weeks. Kipp des-

perately wanted the Blackfeet trade and told his men to hold off returning fire. He loaded his small cannon with Minié balls or grape shot and fired into a grove of cottonwood trees, sending one huge tree crashing to the ground. The Indians scattered. Two of their braver chiefs returned to parley, and admitted to Kipp that Hudson's Bay men to the north had persuaded them to attack the fort. This admission confirmed the suspicions American fur trappers and traders had held for years, that Hudson's Bay was behind a lot of the trouble with the Indians. The Bloods were impressed and profitable trade was resumed.

By spring of 1832 the supply of trade goods was exhausted. Kipp decided to re-

Joseph Kipp is representative of what the trade became in the 1870s—a mixed-blood second-generation trader following in the footsteps of his father, James Kipp. The Kipp family still lives in Montana.

The site of American Fur Company's Fort McKenzie along the Missouri River north of Fort Benton in Chouteau County.
F. LEE GRAVES

turn to Fort Union to replenish his dwindling supplies and to leave a small contingent of men behind to "hold the fort." His men were unwilling to remain in dangerous Blackfeet country, so Fort Piegan was abandoned. The Blackfeet burned the post as soon as the men left.

It was common for American Fur Company men as well as other company men and free trappers to attend the annual rendezvous. Several American Fur Company men attended the rendezvous of 1832 held in Pierre's Hole (north of Driggs, Idaho, near Tetonia) west of Jackson Hole, Wyoming. The rendezvous was lively enough, for the Blackfeet attacked, and the Battle of Pierre's Hole gave everyone plenty of excitement.

Following the rendezvous, brigades departed in different directions. As was a usual practice, American Fur Company brigades tailed Rocky Mountain brigades to find out where their prime, and usually secret, trapping grounds were located. Henry Vanderburgh and Andrew Drips left the rendezvous August 2, following Jim Bridger and Tom Fitzpatrick of the Rocky Mountain Fur Company. Bridger and Fitzpatrick knew they were being followed and led the American Fur Company brigade on a circuitous tour of parts

of Idaho, Wyoming and Montana. At Three Forks they decided to separate, Drips going up the Gallatin and Vanderburgh with 50 men up the Madison.

Vanderburgh crossed over into the Jefferson drainage and ended up on the Ruby River. On October 14 he camped near Sheridan, Montana, and received reports from hunters about a freshly killed buffalo cow just ahead and a campfire still burning by the carcass. Vanderburgh and six men went to investigate. Just as Vanderburgh reached a defile about 50 yards from the river, his party was attacked by over 100 Blackfeet warriors. Vanderburgh was shot off his horse and tomahawked, and a Frenchman named Pilou also was killed. The remaining group, including wounded Warren Angus Ferris who later detailed the story in a journal, returned to the main camp and spread the alarm. Pilou was buried near where he fell, and Vanderburgh's body was never recovered.

The remaining party of 48 reunited with Drips and his men on October 20 on the Beaverhead River at Clark Canyon Dam (Hap Hawkins Lake) at their cache site. The trappers remained at this site four days and then went up Horse Prairie and over into the Salmon River area to trade. Within a year, at Fort Union, Black-

F. LEE GRAVES

feet Chief Eagle Rib showed pistols to artist George Catlin that presumably were taken from Vanderburgh and scalps taken from other white trappers.

Many historians blame Jim Bridger and Tom Fitzpatrick for deliberately leading Vanderburgh's party into a massacre, and the Rocky Mountain men even have been accused of setting up the affair. Like many other stories from the mountains, the complete story of the Vanderburgh Massacre never will be known. Within a few days of the Vanderburgh Massacre,

while Jim Bridger was trapping with Tom Fitzpatrick and his brigade at Three Forks, he picked up two Blackfeet arrowheads in his back in a skirmish. One was removed by Fitzpatrick, but the other three-inch metal trade point he carried in his carcass until it was removed by missionary Dr. Marcus Whitman on the Oregon Trail three years later.

In the fall of 1832 two fur forts were built by the American Fur Company, which extended the arms of Fort Union farther up both the Missouri and Yellow-

Mackinac Island, Michigan. Headquarters of the Northern Department of John Jacob Astor's American Fur Company as well as fur warehouse, and home of Ramsay Crooks and Robert Stuart.

Fort Union

Fort Union was founded in 1829 by Kenneth McKenzie on behalf of the Upper Missouri Outfit of the American Fur Company. The fort played a significant role in the history of the West until the early 1860s. The location was ideal, on the Missouri River upstream about five miles from its junction with the Yellowstone River. The prime site had everything: proximity to both major upstream channels; an abundance of firewood and construction wood; a picturesque setting in a wide, open plain safe from surprise attack; above the flood plain of the Missouri River but close to the water for use and control; and abundant local game.

Through the years Fort Union developed into a favorite visiting spot for dignitaries, many from foreign countries. It was a natural evolution from small trading fort into full-fledged commercial operation taking in thousands of dollars of beaver pelts, and eventually, buffalo robes. Above St. Louis, especially in the Upper Missouri, Fort Union was the center of white civilization.

Within three years of founding Fort Union, the managers realized the importance of getting closer to the prime beaver grounds of the Yellowstone River and Missouri River in central and western Montana. From Fort Union, they extended their reach to these areas through Fort Cass on the Yellowstone River at the mouth of the Big Horn near Hysham, and Fort McKenzie on the Missouri River near present Fort Benton. Both satellite operations answered to Fort Union; from Fort Union they got their supplies and shipped their furs downriver to St. Louis's markets and warehouses.

At 220 feet by 240 feet, Fort Union was fairly large. Its location was a windy one, and on December 14, 1833, a fierce wind blew down two sides of the palisades. They were rebuilt, this time 20 feet high, and dug into the ground resting on a limestone base several feet below the surface. Abundant local cottonwoods were used in construction. A walkway was built around the fort using an "X" pattern for support, which increased stability of the palisades as well. Two square bastions were at the northeast and southwest corners of Fort Union, and its front gate faced the Missouri River.

Besides functioning as observations posts, the bastions served as storage and sleeping quarters. George Catlin even used one of the bastions as his studio during his visit in 1832. To paint, he sometimes sat on one of the 12-pound cannons, which looked out the fort from the porthole. (In 86 days on the Missouri, Catlin produced over 135 pictures.) Around the palisades were log buildings—storage areas, trading room, an ice house, and living quarters for the men. A powder magazine built of hewn stone was capable of storing 50,000 pounds of powder.

On the north side of the courtyard not far from the palisade facing the front gate is the house of the bourgeois, or manager. The two-story frame house had a "widow's walk" on the top center of the roof. At times, imported cognac and fine wines were served at the bourgeois' table, but the average employee was not so fortunate in his bill of fare.

A garden was a source of vegetables for the fort, although Prince Maximilian of Wied remarked in 1833, "Vegetables did not thrive, but mosquitoes did." The garden was near

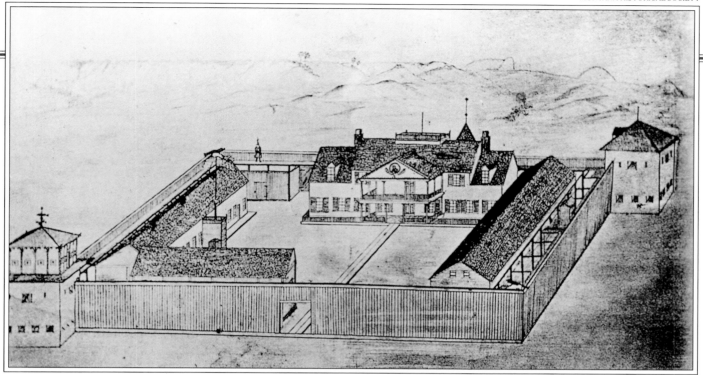

Drawing of Fort Union in 1864.

"Garden Coulee," still visible today. Hunters provided the fort with game, primarily buffalo, but many antelope and deer were taken. On one festive occasion beef was served; the men ate politely, but could not wait to get back to real meat—buffalo.

The first steamboat to reach Fort Union was the *Yellow Stone* in 1832, its arrival revolutionizing the fur trade. Furs, especially heavy buffalo robes, could be transported to St. Louis markets and warehouses more cheaply, faster, and more safely than in smaller keelboats or mackinaws. Visitors, many of them vacationers such as German Prince Maximilian of Wied, could travel on steamboats in comfortable style and were enthralled with life on the frontier.

With the decline of the beaver trade, the buffalo trade was waxing in importance. Fort Union easily made the transition from beaver to buffalo. Fort Union also was a stopping off point for travelers going farther west. In 1866, Montana miner Granville Stuart stopped over at Fort Union as he traveled west. He made a sketch of the fort and noted in his journal that the fort had "sort of a 'played out' look, and is evidently on the decline." Photographs taken of Fort Union at that time bear this record out. Eventually buffalo too declined, and in 1867 the United States Army purchased Fort Union, formally ending its fur-trade history. The fort was dismantled, and its lumber was used to construct Fort Buford, the army post built a short distance downriver.

Fort Union, once described as the crown jewel of the fur trade, lay forgotten on the Montana-North Dakota prairie for nearly 100 years. In 1966 Fort Union Trading Post National Historic Site was established as a unit of the National Park Service System. Historic sketches and descriptions were used to reconstruct Fort Union as it was in 1851. Details were followed so closely that even irregular side boards and windows on the bourgeois' house as shown on original sketches were included. The bourgeois' house is the park headquarters and has a museum, archives and small bookstore. Although the fort actually rests in the state of North Dakota, about one-third of the park complex is in Montana. Fort Union today truly reflects the American fur trade and its role in the opening of the West.

Above: Interior of Fort Union.
Below: Fort Union, built in 1829 on the Montana-North Dakota border, is currently administered by the National Park Service as Fort Union Trading Post National Historic Site. Shown is the house of the bourgeois (manager), which serves as park headquarters and museum.

Fall colors underscore Pilot Peak.

stone rivers into prime beaver grounds. Samuel Tullock went up the Yellowstone from Fort Union for the express purpose of building a trading post among the Crows. Tullock—called Crane by the Indians because of his tall, thin frame—built Fort Cass on the south side of the Yellowstone near the mouth of the Big Horn River near Hysham. It was named for Secretary of War Lewis Cass.

Fort Cass had the reputation of being an extremely dangerous post. In spite of this being Crow country, the Blackfeet ranged through the area. Some of the trappers at the small fort were even apprehensive about going out for firewood. Fort Cass lasted only three years, being replaced in 1835 by Fort Van Buren near the mouth of the Rosebud River near Forsyth. From Fort Van Buren, Charles Larpenteur conducted trade with the Crow Indians, and led brigades up the Big Horn River and its tributaries, trapping and exploring along the way, and noting many of his exploits in an interesting journal. One of his tamer accounts is of having a couple of milk cows with his men on the Yellowstone River and of those big, old rough-and-tumble trappers relishing the fresh, foamy—and undoubtedly warm—milk.

The area between Hysham and Forsyth, Montana, saw several other fur posts between 1835 and 1860: Fort Alexander from 1842 to 1850; Fort Sarpy No. 1 from 1850 to 1855; and Fort Sarpy No. 2 from 1857 to 1860. The forts were small and miserable places to live. Fort Sarpy No. 2 was the last post built for trade with the Crows and was short-lived because the Sioux pushed the Crows westward out of the area and began causing havoc with the post. In the early 1860s the trade in the Big Horn country generally was abandoned.

Fort McKenzie was built on the north side of the Missouri River about six miles above the mouth of the Marias River, fifteen miles northeast of Fort Benton. This post, built in 1832, was one of the largest American Fur Company posts in existence; it flourished eleven years. Alexander Culbertson succeeded Kenneth McKenzie as manager of the Upper Missouri Outfit. To him is due the immense success of Fort McKenzie. Culbertson was married to the beautiful Blackfeet Natawista, which politically helped relations with the Blackfeet. Trade flourished, and relations with the often-hostile Blackfeet improved, that is, until 1844. Alexander Culbertson was transferred by the company to Fort Laramie, which left F.A. Chardon in charge at Fort McKenzie. Chardon's black slave, Tom Reese, was killed by Blackfeet angry because they were refused gifts at the fort. Chardon and a ne'er-do-well friend of his named Alexander Harvey plotted revenge. They decided to retaliate and murder the first group of Blackfeet that came to the fort. On February 19, 1844, a group of peaceful Blackfeet including women and children appeared at Fort McKenzie to trade. They were allowed to enter through the gate and were immediately fired upon. Four Indians were killed outright and seventeen were wounded. Harvey rushed out braining any wounded with an ax, leaving a total of twenty-one dead. The slaughter resulted in the men being afraid to remain in the area, so Fort McKenzie was abandoned, then burned as the trappers left.

The men relocated downriver near the mouth of the Judith River, calling their new post Fort Chardon. The American Fur Company immediately felt a loss of revenue because the Indians refused to trade there, coming only to harass the fort. Pierre Chouteau summoned Alexander Culbertson to New York and charged him to return to the Upper Missouri, restore peace, and resume a profitable trade with the Indians. Culbertson returned to Fort Chardon in the spring of 1845, immediately relieved Harvey and burned the fort. He built Fort Cotton fif-

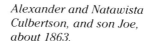

Alexander and Natawista Culbertson, and son Joe, about 1863.

teen miles upriver, but its location proved unsatisfactory and was abandoned shortly.

In 1846 Culbertson relocated again, this time at the present site of Fort Benton, first calling his new post Fort Clay, then Fort Lewis. By 1848 American Fur Company officials called the new masterpiece Fort Benton, after avid fur-trade supporter and Missouri senator Thomas Hart Benton. Christmas night of 1850 bourgeois Alexander Culbertson made the name change official. For the next decade Culbertson remained at Fort Benton and ran a profitable operation that, in the opinion of some historians, surpassed Fort Union in its importance to the fur trade.

The first steamboat to reach Fort Union was the *Yellow Stone*, in 1832; the first to reach Fort Benton was the *Chippewa*, in 1860. Prior to that time, furs were taken downstream to Fort Union primarily on keelboats that could haul a heavy cargo as well as provide protection for the men. When the first steamer reached Fort Benton, the entire transportation system to the Upper Missouri was revolutionized. The advent of the steamboat brought speed, safety for cargo, and a capability for heavier loads, which boosted the dwindling beaver-fur trade and the expanding buffalo-robe trade. In 1860, steamboats began bringing merchandise upriver and returning with goods and furs from the mountains. This method continued until the railroads made the river route unprofitable. The St. Paul, Minneapolis and Manitoba Railroad reached Fort Benton September 28, 1887, essentially ending steamboat navigation on the Missouri.

By the year 1850 the beaver-fur trade was effectively over in Montana. The last rendezvous was held in 1840 on the Green River in Wyoming. No company, big or small, would be able to profit by

Fort Benton

Fort Benton on the Missouri (not to be confused with Fort Benton on the Yellowstone) was founded by the American Fur Company in 1847, construction having begun in late 1846. The structure was built of cottonwood, and by 1850 adobe was used for bastions and walls. Its location was on the north side of the Missouri River about 2,500 miles above St. Louis and about 500 miles above Fort Union. The area was prized for trade with the Blackfeet Indians, and several short-lived forts had sprung up and faded away there since the early 1830s.

The post first was called Fort Clay and then Fort Lewis. In St. Louis, American Fur Company officials called the new Blackfeet post Fort Benton, after Senator Thomas Hart Benton. Christmas night of 1850, bourgeois Alexander Culbertson told his men that they were spending their last Christmas at Fort Lewis and their first Christmas at Fort Benton.

Fort Benton missed much of the early beaver trade, but got in on the apex of the buffalo-robe trade. With the coming of the first steamboat, the *Chippewa,* in 1860, Fort Benton sprang from a rough-and-tumble town to a center of commerce and trade. Fort Benton became the steamboat head for the Missouri River, with as many as 54 steamboats arriving in 1878, and as many as 32 in 1866. The peak years of 1875, 1876 and 1878 saw 75,000 buffalo robes transported downriver from Fort Benton aboard steamboats. (For some reason, 1877 saw a dip to 50,000 robes.) This profitable mode of transportation continued until 1887 when the St. Paul, Minneapolis and Manitoba Railroad arrived. The "iron horse" put the steamboat out of business and introduced yet another era of commerce and transportation.

Fort Benton supplied many of the goods to the boom-and-bust towns founded at the time—Bannack in 1862, Virginia City in 1863, and Last Chance Gulch (Helena) in 1864. Other goods were supplied by freight wagons from Salt Lake City. Between 1858 and 1862 John Mullan sited the Mullan Road, designed to take the place of the nonexistent inland waterway. Connecting Fort

F. LEE GRAVES

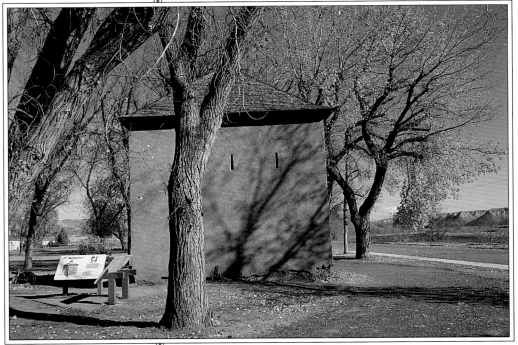

Facing page: *Built in the early 1850s out of adobe, the blockhouse at historic old Fort Benton on the Missouri River stands in the city park.*

Left: *The interior of a fur trapper's cabin is part of the museum at Fort Benton.*
Below: *Blockhouse interior, Fort Benton.*

F. LEE GRAVES PHOTOS

Benton with Fort Walla Walla on the Columbia River would link the Atlantic with the Pacific.

The buffalo-robe trade began to decline in the late 1860s. The American Fur Company closed its fur operation at Fort Benton in 1870 and leased the fort to the government. Since 1864, Fort Benton has been the seat Chouteau County. All that remains of the old fort is one blockhouse and part of an adobe wall protected by a screen enclosure. The town sports an attractive museum with a well-documented, interesting section on the fur trade. The museum also is home to the Hornaday buffalo group, the lead bull of which was the model for the buffalo-head nickel, the Wyoming state flag, and several U.S. postage stamps.

Fort Benton was the head of steam navigation on the Missouri River. Sketch by Gustavus Sohon (1825-1903).

bringing goods to the mountains to trade. Men sensed that the days of the beaver trade were numbered. When John Jacob Astor visited London in 1833, he noticed that fashions were changing and wrote, "I very much fear beaver will not sell well very soon unless very fine. It appears that they make hats out of silk in place of beaver." How prophetic he was, but the phoenix rising from the ashes of the beaver-fur trade was the buffalo-robe trade, destined to a short life.

By 1860 the American Fur Company had discontinued trade on the Yellowstone. In 1867 the government purchased Fort Union and dismantled it to build military Fort Buford east of there. Fort Benton was purchased by the military in 1869. Officially it was the end of a fabulous era.

Mountain man Robert Newell summed it up when he told his friend Joe Meek:

"We are done with this life in the mountains—done with wading in beaver streams, and freezing or starving alternately—done with Indian trading and Indian fighting. The fur trade is dead in the Rocky Mountains, and it is no place for us now, if it ever was. We are young yet and have life before us. We cannot waste it here; we cannot or will not return to the states."

Boats of the Fur Trade

Bullboat. The bullboat was a popular mode of transportation on the Upper Missouri because it was light, easy to make, and carried a large load when necessary. This bowl-shaped boat was made of bent willow sticks lashed together for stability. The sticks were covered over with hides sewn together, buffalo being the hide of choice because of its size and availability. The seams were then sealed with pitch, making a waterproof container. The craft could be made as large as needed and could carry up to three or four persons and a good-sized cargo. Bullboats could, however, tip over easily; they also were slow and steering was not easy.

Dugout. A dugout is a canoe made from a tree which is "dug out" or hollowed out. (A canoe oftentimes is made of a framework covered with hides or bark.) Cottonwood trees were the most often used because they were plentiful in the Upper Missouri. The cottonwoods were long and straight, and were soft enough to hollow out easily, but strong enough to last a long time. The tree was chopped down, tapered at the ends and hollowed out by chopping and burning. The bottoms were about two inches thick and the sides were about one inch thick. The most practical length was about fifteen feet. A dugout was easily controlled even by one man. Dugouts were speedy and moved silently over the water. Propulsion was by paddle, but a pole also could be used.

Keelboat. A keelboat was up to seventy feet long and had a five-foot-high cargo box that ran practically from stem to stern. Simply put, a keelboat was a box on a hull. Width varied with length; a boat sixty feet in length was about eighteen feet at its widest point. A high mast was slightly forward of center. Keelboats were propelled by sail, poles or cordelle, which was a long rope used to pull the craft upstream. A heavy keel ran from stem to stern (covered over with planks); hence the name. At the height of the fur trade, there were an estimated 3,000 keelboats in use on the rivers.

Mackinaw. The mackinaw was a flat-bottomed boat constructed of rough-cut lumber and often fifty feet in length. The large heavy boat was used only once. A mackinaw was built where needed to transport furs and other goods downstream, and then abandoned. Four oarsmen in the bow and a tiller at the stern were the only crew needed. The load—sometimes up to fifteen tons—was placed between the oarsmen and tiller.

Pirogue. The pirogue was constructed by lashing together two or more dugouts, which were then covered over with a floor. The sides were built up in some manner, either with boards or poles. Propulsion was by sails, oars or poles. The pirogue could carry a heavy cargo and was used for both upstream and downstream travel.

Left: Traps, scraper and castoreum bottle were essential tools of the fur trade.
Below: Winter scene of a beaver stream south of the Scapegoat Wilderness Area, west of Lincoln.

Facing page: Fairly common in the West, lodgepole pine wickiups are usually found in stands of timber. This wickiup, located in Beaverhead County, was used by the Tukudika Shoshone and is about 200 years old. F. LEE GRAVES

F. LEE GRAVES

What Became of the Mountain Man?

The mountain men, toward the end of the beaver trade in the late 1830s, realized that their glorious way of life was ending. Many felt frustrated because they were not skilled in any other work. Others were not as spry as they once were. They all had to decide what to do with the rest of their lives.

Some stayed on and were absorbed by the buffalo trade. When the robe trade waned, they trapped otter, fox, coyote, marten, bobcat, mountain lion, as well as beaver. Most men, however, moved out of the Rocky Mountains, forced to look for other work. A few married and started families. Many went to farm in Oregon or California, or worked as traders and sutlers at a fort or post along one of the many trails heading west.

Charles Larpenteur wrote his memoirs, published today as *Forty Years a Fur Trader on the Upper Missouri*. Kit Carson began an entirely new career, guiding for the U.S. Army in the Southwest. Other men went into law enforcement, learned skills such as blacksmithing and tin making, or went into the freight or mercantile business. "Liver Eatin'" Johnson retired from the fur business and became the sheriff of Carbon County, Montana, where he lived to ripe old age. Robert Newell lamented in his memoirs that about fifteen of his compatriots of the mountains were on their way to California to advance their careers in horse stealing.

Many trappers lived a long time after their romantic, but difficult, forays into the Rocky Mountains after furs. Perhaps the fortunate ones were Jedediah Smith and Henry Vanderburgh, who were killed quickly while happily pursuing their lifelong endeavor; they did not have to witness the end, as did Old Gabe, Jim Bridger who died blind on July 17, 1881. In Stanley Vestal's book *Jim Bridger, Mountain Man*, the chapter "The End of the Trail" sadly sums up the fate of many of the once-dashing D'Artagnans of the mountains: "But in spite of the new friends about him, the old man sometimes grew very lonely. He longed to talk to some of his comrades of the beaver trail...'But I know I will not be able to see any of my oldtime mountain friends any more. I know that my time is near.' So, old and blind and poor, he sat on his porch with sightless eyes towards the West, with his square face and close-cropped beard, which reminded visitors of president Grant—with his tall, lank frame and the shawl about his shoulders, which reminded people of President Lincoln—sat and waited for the end."

Fort Alexander. Built in November 1842 by Charles Larpenteur and Alexander McKenzie at the mouth of Armell's Creek (junction of I-94 and Colstrip Road, Highway 39) west of Forsyth. Lasted until 1850.

Fort Benton on the Missouri. Built in 1847 by Major Alexander Culbertson of the American Fur Company on the Missouri River for Blackfeet trade. Has the reputation of being the most important of all the fur-trade forts. Purchased by the government in 1869 and became a military fort.

Fort Benton on the Yellowstone. Constructed during the fall of 1821 on the Yellowstone River by Joshua Pilcher of Missouri Fur Company on or near the site of Fort Manuel Lisa west of Hysham.

Fort Campbell. An "opposition" trading post of Harvey, Primeau and Company where Fort Benton is located now. Built by Alexander Harvey in 1846, the log stockade first was on the south side of the river. Shortly thereafter it was removed to the north side and built of adobe. Abandoned in 1860.

Fort Cass. Built by Samuel Tullock in 1832 for the American Fur Company. The location is very near the Yellowstone-Treasure County line two miles east of Custer, Montana. A 130-foot-square cottonwood log fort with two blockhouses at opposite corners. Abandoned in 1835.

Fort F.A. Chardon. Built in 1844 by Alexander Harvey and Chardon, acting for American Fur Company, near mouth of the Judith River on the Missouri River. Abandoned by Culbertson the next year.

Fort Connah. Construction was begun in 1846 by Angus McDonald of Hudson's Bay Company. It was the last Hudson's Bay Company post constructed in U.S. territory. Named for the Connen River in Scotland. Closed by 1871. All that remains is one log storehouse 6 miles south of Ronan.

Fort Cotton. Established in 1844 by the American Fur Company three miles above Fort Benton. Lasted less than a year.

Flathead Post. Established in 1823 by Alexander Ross of Hudson's Bay Company about five miles east of Thompson Falls.

This post possibly was moved several times through the years. In 1846 it was removed to Post Creek near Charlo and renamed Fort Connah.

Fort Henry. (See also Three Forks Post.) Another Fort Henry was founded by Andrew Henry during the winter of 1810-11 on the Henry's (North) Fork of the Snake River in Idaho.

Fort Howse. Built in 1810 by Hudson's Bay trader, Joseph Howse. Occupied during the winter and abandoned in the spring of 1811. Location was Flathead Valley, exact site unknown.

Fort Jackson. Built in 1833 as a winter camp by F.A. Chardon in December 1833 at mouth of Poplar River where Poplar, Montana is located today. Its palisade was about 50 feet square.

Kootenai Post. Established in November 1808 by Finan McDonald of the North West Company on the Kootenai River nearly opposite the present town of Libby. The post consisted of two leather lodges and a log building. Location moved in 1811 to near Jennings, Montana. Date of closure unknown.

Fort Lewis. Established in 1845 on the Missouri River about 18 miles northeast of Fort Benton. This American Fur Company fort was dismantled in 1847 and moved to the site of Fort Benton.

Fort Manuel Lisa. Established in 1807 by Manuel Lisa at the mouth of the Big Horn River near Hysham. This was the first permanent settlement in Montana and was occupied until 1811. Also called Fort Remon (after Lisa's son), Fort Raymond, Fort Manuel Lisa, and Fort Manuel.

Fort McKenzie. Built by the American Fur Company in 1832 on the north bank of the Missouri River about 14 miles upriver, northeast of Fort Benton. One of the largest of the American Fur Company posts, it was abandoned in 1844.

Fort Pease. A minor, temporary trading post built in 1875 by Major F.D. Pease for trade with the Crows. Its stockade was 100 feet square and was located on the north bank of the Yellowstone River sev-

Scenes from a modern-day mountain man rendezvous—percussion rifle, Kentucky long rifle and pouch.

Facing Page: *Bond Creek, a small beaver stream in Beaverhead County with Mount Torrey (11,176 feet) capping the spring scene.*

en miles below the mouth of the Big Horn River near Hysham. In March of 1876 soldiers from Fort Ellis at Bozeman forced the post to close because of increasing danger from Sioux Indians.

Fort Piegan. Built by James Kipp of the American Fur Company in the spring of 1831 near the mouth of the Marias River on the Missouri near Loma. The 110-foot-square, 25-foot-high cottonwood palisade was abandoned in the spring of 1832.

Salish House. Built by David Thompson of the North West Company in November 1809. Its location was on the Clark's Fork of the Columbia near Thompson Falls.

Fort Sarpy No. 1. Built in 1850 by the American Fur Company for trade with the Crows. The post was located on the north bank of the Yellowstone about five miles below the mouth of the Rosebud River near Rosebud, Montana, fifteen miles east of Forsyth. Abandoned and burned May 19, 1855.

Fort Sarpy No. 2. The last post built for trade with the Crow Indians. Built in 1857 by Alexander Culbertson of the American Fur Company on the Yellowstone River about 25 miles below the mouth of the Big Horn River near present-day Sanders. It was about 100 feet square and consisted of a palisade of 15-foot-high cottonwood logs.

Three Forks Post. Also called Fort Henry. Built by Andrew Henry and Pierre Menard of the Missouri Fur Company near Three Forks, Montana, between the Jefferson and Madison rivers about two miles above their confluence. Construction began April 3, 1810. The post lasted until the late fall of 1810 and was abandoned because of tremendous Blackfeet pressure. The 300-foot-square, 3-foot-deep double-row palisade was built of cottonwood logs.

Fort Union. Built by the American Fur Company in 1829, probably overseen by James Kipp. The 220-foot by 240-foot palisade of cottonwood logs was set on bedrock of limestone. The location of the primary post of the American Fur Company is on the Montana-North Dakota border and on the north bank of the Missouri River near its confluence with the Yellowstone River. Last used as a fur fort in 1867 and then purchased by the U.S. military.

Fort Van Buren. Built by Samuel Tullock in 1835 near the mouth of Rosebud Creek east of Forsyth. This American Fur Company post was abandoned and burned in 1842 by Charles Larpenteur.

Rendezvous Sites

1825	Randazvouze Creek	Located about four miles west of McKinnon, Wyoming, on Henry's Fork River. Ashley's journal gives the date July 1 and lists about 129 men present.
1826	Willow Valley	Cache Valley—also called Willow Valley—near Logan, Utah. A few days after the rendezvous ended, the Henry-Ashley Firm (Rocky Mountain Fur Company) sold out to Jedediah Smith, David Jackson and William Sublette.
1827	Sweet Lake	South end of Bear Lake in Utah near Laketown. The gathering lasted about two weeks in July with over 300 in attendance.
1828	Sweet Lake	As in 1827, the event started in a battle with the Blackfeet. Robert Campbell, just in from the Flathead Valley, was attacked a few miles north of the rendezvous site; he lost one man and $5,000 worth of furs.
1829	Popo Agie	The first of two rendezvous in 1829 prearranged by William Sublette, who was bringing a supply train from St. Louis. The site was on the Popo Agie River about a mile east of Lander, Wyoming. Over $22,000 worth of beaver exchanged hands in the July gathering.
1829	Pierre's Hole	Considered the major rendezvous of the year. Held in August in Pierre's Hole—now Teton Basin—near Tetonia and Driggs, Idaho. Over 175 men attended.
1830	Wind River	Ten wagons each pulled by five mules hauling over $30,000 worth of goods supplied this gathering, which was on the Wind River about two miles northeast of Riverton, Wyoming. At this rendezvous, on August 4, Jedediah Smith, David Jackson, and William Sublette sold out their interests to Fraeb, Gervais, Bridger, Fitzpatrick and Milton Sublette, beginning the third phase of the Rocky Mountain Fur Company.

1831 Willow Valley	This September rendezvous appears to have been uneventful.
1832 Pierre's Hole	This July event was the largest ever, with over 1,000 trappers attending; the men began to gather in June. In addition to Rocky Mountain Fur Company and free trappers, several other companies were represented, including the American Fur Company, Hudson's Bay Company, and many small independent companies. There were separate camps because of the intense rivalry.
	As the rendezvous began to break up on July 7, Blackfeet attacked, and the Battle of Pierre's Hole ensued.
	William Sublette transported the furs—nearly 14,000 pounds at 50¢ per pound—to St. Louis by way of Teton Pass, arriving in St. Louis on October 3.
	From this rendezvous, the American Fur Company followed the Rocky Mountain Fur Company to learn their trapping grounds and methods, which led to the Vanderburgh Massacre on October 14 near Sheridan, Montana.
1833 Green River	At the junction of the Green River and Horse Creek near Daniel, Wyoming. In July, the American Fur Company and Rocky Mountain Fur Company held their rendezvous near Fort Bonneville about five miles apart. The rendezvous ended July 24.
	Excitement in the mountains always came in varied forms. This time, rabid wolves attacked one of the camps, biting several people, who subsequently died of hydrophobia.
1834 Ham's Fork	Near Granger, Wyoming, are the four sites of the 1834 rendezvous of the American Fur Company and the Rocky Mountain Fur Company on the Ham's Fork River. Each company moved its original location upstream for better animal pasture. On June 20, the Rocky Mountain Fur Company dissolved, with each partner taking a share of the dissolution profits.
1835 Green River	Visitors to this August event were missionaries Dr. Marcus Whitman and Samuel Parker, as well as a large number of Indians and Hudson's Bay trappers.
1836 Green River	Guests this year included Dr. Whitman, his new bride Narcissa, and the Rev. and Mrs. Henry Spaulding on their way to Oregon to bring the Indians the message of the Christian God. The caravan from St. Louis reached the site on July 6, meeting such mountain men as Kit Carson, Osborne Russell, Joe Meek, and several Hudson's Bay trappers under John McLeod.
1837 Green River	Accompanying the supply train led by Thomas "Broken Hand" Fitzpatrick were Etienne Provost (for whom Provo, Utah, is named), and Alfred Jacob Miller, who painted much of the fur-trade life and places, becoming one of the most famous artists of the American West.
1838 Wind River	The same site as the 1830 rendezvous. Andrew Drips commanded the supply train that fueled the trappers for the event, which commenced June 23. Among the spectators at the gathering was August Johann Sutter—of Sutter's Mill fame in California gold-rush history—on his way west.
	A Hudson's Bay Company account shows only 125 trappers present, and only about 2,000 pelts taken in by the American Fur Company.
1839 Green River	This July rendezvous was attended by Francis Ermatinger, bourgeois of Fort Hall (Pocatello), and fourteen of his men. Kit Carson brought furs trapped from the Upper Missouri in Montana; he also brought Robert Newell, Andrew Drips, and several missionaries.
	Most of the participants began to recognize that the way of life they had enjoyed for the past several years quickly was coming to an end.
1840 Green River	The last of the famous gatherings of the trappers. Andrew Drips, Jim Bridger, and Henry Fraeb guided the last supply train from St. Louis to the rendezvous—30 wagons and about 40 men. On June 30, the caravan arrived, bringing among the suppliers Jesuit priest Pierre-Jean DeSmet, who left a comprehensive journal of the event.

Data from Gowans' *Rocky Mountain Rendezvous: A History of the Fur Trade Rendezvous.*

Fur Trade Vocabulary

Bourgeois	Manager of a trading post.
Bullboat	Bowl-shaped boat made of bent willows and covered with buffalo hides.
Cordelle	Rope or line used to pull a keelboat.
Dugout	Wooden canoe—sometimes 60 or 70 feet long and 4 feet across—hollowed out of a log.
Engagé	Individual who signed a contract of employment for wages as a boatman or hunter. One hired.
Factor	Trader.
Factory	Trading house or fur fort used primarily for trading.
Free trapper	An individual who had not bound himself to serve any man or company while in the mountains.
Hole	Valley.
Keelboat	Sixty feet long and with a 5-foot-high cargo box that ran practically from stem to stern. Propelled by sail, poles or cordelle.
Mackinaw	Heavy boat, often fifty feet long. Built upriver and used for one trip downriver.
Opposition	An American Fur Company term meaning all other competing fur companies.
Partisan	The leader of an expedition.
Pirogue	Two or more dugouts lashed together with flooring over the top and the sides built up.
Plew	Beaver pelt.
Possibles	Collection of things an individual needed in the mountains, often kept in a "possibles sack."
Rees	Arikara Indians, *not* the Minatarees.
Rendezvous	Yearly gathering in the mountains of trappers and traders to trade their furs for supplies.
Strike-a-light	Fire-starting device crafted of metal, which produced a spark when struck against flint, serving as the "matches" of the frontier.
Upper Missouri	North of the Big Sioux River at Sioux City, Iowa.
Vermilion	A red cloth valued by the Indians.
Voyageur	Boatman, most often of French-Canadian descent.

For Further Reading

Abbott, Carl Newton. *Montana in the Making.* Billings: Gazette Printing Company, 1964.

Berry, Don. A *Majority of Scoundrels.* Sausalito: Comstock Editions, 1961.

Chittenden, Hiram Martin. *American Fur Trade of the Far West, Vol. 2.* First publication 1902. Lincoln: University of Nebraska Press, 1986.

Dale, Harrison C. *Explorations of William H. Ashley and Jedediah Smith, 1822-1829.* Lincoln: University of Nebraska Press, 1991.

DeVoto, Bernard. *Across the Wide Missouri.* Cambridge: Riverside Press, 1947.

Ferris, Warren Angus. *Life in the Rocky Mountains.* Denver: Old West Publishing Company, 1940.

Gowans, Fred R. *Rocky Mountain Rendezvous.* Layton: Gibbs M. Smith, 1985.

Hafen, Leroy. *Broken Hand: The Life of Thomas Fitzpatrick—Mountain Man, Guide and Indian Agent.* Lincoln: University of Nebraska Press, 1981.

Hafen, Leroy R. and Ann, eds. *The Mountain Men and the Fur Trade of the Far West.* 10 vols. Glendale: Arthur H. Clark, 1965.

Kurz, Rudolph Friederich. *Journal of Rudolph Friederich Kurz.* Fairfield: Lincoln: University of Nebraska, 1970.

Larpenteur, Charles. *Forty Years a Fur Trader on the Upper Missouri.* Lincoln: University of Nebraska Press, 1989.

Laycock, George. *The Mountain Men.* Danbury: Outdoor Life Books, 1988.

Miller, Don, and Stan Cohen. *Military and Trading Posts of Montana.* Missoula: Pictorial Histories, 1978.

Montana: The Magazine of Western History: Various volumes and issues.

Newman, Peter C. *A Company of Adventurers.* Markham: Viking Studio Books, 1985.

Newman. *Caesars of the Wilderness.* Markham: Viking Studio Books, 1987.

Newman. *Empire of the Bay.* Markham: Viking Studio Books, 1989.

Oglesby, Richard E. *Manuel Lisa and the Opening of the Missouri Fur Trade.* Norman: University Of Oklahoma Press, 1963.

Overholser, Joel. *Fort Benton: World's Innermost Port.* Fort Benton: Joel Overholser, 1987.

Phillips, Paul C. *The Fur Trade.* 2 vols. Norman: University of Oklahoma, 1961.

Thompson, Erwin N. *Fort Union Trading Post.* Medora: Theodore Roosevelt Nature and History Association, 1986.

Vestal, Stanley. *Jim Bridger: Mountain Man.* Lincoln: University of Nebraska Press, 1970.

Wisart, David J. *The Fur Trade of the American West.* Lincoln: University of Nebraska Press, 1979.

Index